DELAWARE VALLEY REGIONAL BUSINESS ASSISTANCE

A Guide to Business Assistance in the Delaware Valley

A Business Resource Guide

Calvin R. Tucker

A GUIDE TO BUSINESS ASSISTANCE IN THE DELAWARE VALLEY REGION

A Business Resource Guide

Written & Published by Calvin R. Tucker,

Philadelphia, Pennsylvania

A GUIDE TO BUSINESS ASSISTANCE IN THE DELAWARE VALLEY REGION

© 2019 Calvin R. Tucker, Philadelphia, Pennsylvania

ISBN: 978-0-578-84666-8

Publisher's Note

As a business owner and consultant to business, I often have the occasion to offer advice on which loans are right for a particular business, which technical assistance advisor to choose for a specific skill set and where to find business or executive training, because these issues seem to be consistent across all small business, I decided to write this guide to help with this challenge. In 1980, as a consultant, I authored a similar version of the guide for the City of Philadelphia, "A Guide to Business Assistance in Philadelphia".

Contents

Matrix of Services

Services by County	Financial	Technical Assistance	Training
Philadelphia, PA	✔	✔	✔
Montgomery County, PA	✔	✔	✔
Delaware County, PA	✔	✔	✔
Chester County, PA	✔	✔	✔
Bucks County, PA	✔	✔	✔
Lancaster County, PA	✔	✔	✔
Wilmington, DE	✔	✔	✔
Reading, PA	✔	✔	✔
Trenton, NJ	✔	✔	✔
Camden, NJ	✔	✔	✔

Philadelphia County

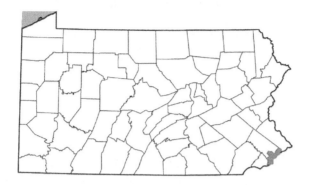

Philadelphia County is the most populous county in the U.S. state of Pennsylvania. As of 2019, Philadelphia County was home to an estimated population of 1,584,064 residents. The county is the second smallest county in Pennsylvania by land area. Philadelphia County is one of the three original counties, along with Chester and Bucks counties, created by William Penn during November 1682. Since 1854, the county has been coextensive with the City of Philadelphia. Philadelphia County is part of the Philadelphia-Camden-Wilmington, PA-NJ-DE-MD (Combined Statistical Area, known as the Delaware Valley), located along the lower Delaware and Schuylkill Rivers, within the Northeast megalopolis. Philadelphia County is the economic and cultural anchor of the Delaware Valley, the ninth-largest combined statistical area in the United States with an estimated population of 7.2 million.

Organizations

West Philadelphia Financial Services Institution (WPFSI)

Address: 5200 Warren Street, Philadelphia, PA 19131,

Telephone: 215-452-0100.

Website: www.wpfsi.com

DESCRIPTION OF SERVICES: CDFI & SBA Micro lender who provides Economic Development, Financial and Technical Assistance Services to businesses in the underserved community.

TYPE OF FINANCING OFFERED: Direct Small business and Micro financing.

LOAN RANGES: $1000 to $100, 000- larger deals as presented.

COST OF FINANCING (FEES): 3% plus application fee.

COLLATERAL REQUIREMENT: Yes.

MINIMUM CREDIT SCORE CONSIDERATION: 600 credit score but will consider lower score with mitigating circumstances.

Entrepreneurs Works

Address: The Bourse Building, 111 S. Independence Mall East, Suite 528, Philadelphia, PA 19106, Telephone: 215-545-3100

DESCRIPTION OF SERVICES: Entrepreneur Works is a nonprofit organization that offers access to microloans, business training, and one-on-one guidance to hundreds of entrepreneurs each year, empowering small business owners from all walks of life to succeed, prosper, and build sustainable communities.

TYPE OF FINANCING OFFERED: Women Entrepreneurs Loan up to $50,000

Special interest rate discount for majority women-owned businesses that have been in operation for two or more years.

Terms of repayment: up to 6 years

Typically used for business expansion, construction/renovation, inventory, working capital, or machinery/equipment.

Small Business Loans up to $50,000

Terms of repayment: up to 6 years)

Typically used for business expansion, construction/renovation, inventory, working capital, or machinery/equipment.

Machinery and Equipment Loans up to $50,000

Terms of repayment: up to 6 years

Typically used for business expansion through the purchase of new equipment (production machinery, computers, vehicles, etc.)

Vendor Loans up to $1,000

Terms of repayment: 6-9 months

Used to cover supplies, permit/booth fees and inventory for a vending event.

LOAN RANGES: $1,000 to $50,000

COST OF FINANCING (FEES): For more information about our loans, please contact our Loan Department at (215) 545-3100 or email us at loans@entre-works.org.

COLLATERAL REQUIREMENT: Yes.

North Philadelphia Financial Partnership, Neighborhood Progress Fund

Address: Liberty Square West Tower, 1300 W. Lehigh Ave, Suite 100, Philadelphia, PA 19132,

Telephone: 215-232-0516 (office) | 215-232-0519 (fax)

Email: info@npfp.org

DESCRIPTION OF SERVICES: Neighborhood Progress Fund believes access to capital is the key to empowering entrepreneurs to play a leading role in the revitalization of their communities, regardless of their economic background. For twenty years, we have helped people in forgotten communities start and grow their businesses by providing loans and business development mentoring. Our approach makes all the difference — We lend a helping hand, too.

TYPE OF FINANCING OFFERED:

Working Capital Loans

To meet some of your company's short-term financial needs, you can take advantage of a working capital loan. This loan is typically repaid within a year and can be used to finance inventory, accounts receivable or any other current asset.

Bridge Loans

Bridge loans can be used as short-term financing to bridge an anticipated or awarded cash source. Many of our bridge loans finance municipal grants or loans that are paid on a reimbursement basis. This loan is typically repaid within a year.

Term Loans

This type of loan is used to finance some of your company's longer term capital expenditure needs. Terms loans can be used to purchase machinery, equipment, furniture, leasehold improvements, commercial vehicles and most other fixed assets excluding real estate.

Business Line of Credit

Instead of borrower a sizable sum of cash, you can opt to open a business line of credit instead. This will allow you to access money as the need arise, like using your credit card.

Commercial Mortgages

Commercial mortgages can be used to finance real estate acquisition and refinancing. These loans are typically secured by real property, such as commercial land, buildings and private residences.

Construction Loans

Construction loans can be used to finance the development and construction of commercial property. These loans are typically secured by real property, such as commercial land, buildings and private residences.

Neighborhood Solution

If you recently started a business, plan to start a business or need help implementing a growth strategy, the Neighborhood Solution could be the answer to your short-term and intermediate financing needs. Terms and conditions are flexible and are based on the entrepreneur's needs.

Beech Capital Venture Corporation

Address: 1510 Cecil B. Moore Avenue, Philadelphia, PA 19121,

Telephone: 215-763-8825

DESCRIPTION OF SERVICES: Beech Business Bank is a loan program managed by the Beech Capital Venture Corporation (BCVC). BCVC is a Certified Development Financial Institution of the

U.S. Department of the Treasury.

Beech Business Bank provides loans to for-profits, non-profit organizations and community development corporations with a primary focus on the economically distressed areas in North, West and Northwest Philadelphia. Beech Business Bank encourages participation by banks and venture capitalists in the financing of businesses and community development corporations.

TYPE OF FINANCING OFFERED: Small business financing Real Estate (purchase for the operation of the owner's business) Machinery and Equipment Furniture and Fixtures Purchase of inventory Working Capital

LOAN RANGES: Maximum Loan is $100,000 or 60% of the Total Project Cost, whichever is less; Minimum Loan is $10,000.

Enterprise Center Capital Corporation

Address: 4548 Market Street, Philadelphia, PA 19139,

Telephone: 215-895-4024

TEC Capital Corporation (TEC-CC) helps finance eligible small businesses that have difficulty obtaining loans for start-up capital and business growth. With a focus on women- and minority-owned businesses, TEC-CC originates loans to entrepreneurs through its status as a CDFI (Community Development Financial Institution) and a U.S. Small Business Administration Microloan Intermediary.

DESCRIPTION OF SERVICES: Stage one represents start-up or early-stage businesses in need of financing of $5,000-$50,000. Stage two are early to mid-stage businesses in need of development and growth capital from $50,000-$100,000. Stage three represents mature businesses seeking access to capital to support contracts and procurement opportunities and in need of financing of more than $100,000.

TYPE OF FINANCING OFFERED: Loans range from $5,000 to $100,000

LOAN RANGES: $5,000 to $100,000

Finanta

Address: 1301 N. 2nd Street, Philadelphia, PA 19122,

Telephone: 267-236-7001

DESCRIPTION OF SERVICES: FINANTA, abbreviation for Financing and Technical Assistance, is a mission-driven nonprofit lending institution facilitating access to capital and credit building services to entrepreneurs, consumers, and first-time homebuyers in the Philadelphia region. FINANTA offers a wide range of products and services, including credit building microloans, affinity group borrowing, business loans and Technical Assistance

TYPE OF FINANCING OFFERED: FINANTA's Affinity Group Lending Program for entrepreneurs provides loans, credit building, and technical assistance to lending circles (known globally as Roscas, Tandas, Susus, and more) and their members who have similar financial needs and desire to establish credit. This product is tailored to the needs of entrepreneurs.

FINANTA's business loans and lines of credit offer fair, flexible, and transparent terms and can be used for a wide variety of business needs.

LOAN RANGES: Loan products range from $50,000 microloans to $250,000 small business loans.

Women's Opportunities Resource Center

Address: 2010 Chestnut Street, Philadelphia, PA 19103,

Telephone: 215-564-5500

DESCRIPTION OF SERVICES: The mission of the Women's Opportunities Resource Center (WORC) is to promote social and economic self-sufficiency primarily for economically disadvantaged women and their families. WORC provides training, individual business assistance, incentive savings program, job placement, and access to business and financial resources. WORC empowers its constituents through various self-help strategies including savings, a self-employment network, and access to its local and national affiliations. Additionally, WORC encourages community awareness and responsiveness concerning issues impacting economic equity and independence.

TYPE OF FINANCING OFFERED: WORC is a U.S. Small Business Administration (SBA) Micro-loan Intermediary and EOF a subsidiary of WORC is a U.S. Department of Treasury Community Development Financial Institution (CDFI). We offer loans, investment products and services to low-income and underserved populations in the Philadelphia Metropolitan Area looking to start or expand their businesses, with a special focus on women and minorities. Products include:

- Credit Builder Loans up to $1,000
- Direct Loan $1,000 to $2,500
- Small Business Loans up to $10,000
- Credit Line up to $20,000
- Expansion Loans up to $50,000

- Assistance with developing business plan and financial projections, market access, graphic design, and professional services (legal, accounting...)
- Referrals to partner banks and community loan funds for business loans and related assistance.

LOAN RANGES: $1,000 to $50,000

United Bank of Philadelphia

Address: 30 South 15th Street, Philadelphia, PA 19102

Telephone: 215-231-3670

DESCRIPTION OF SERVICES: The primary mission of United Bank of Philadelphia is to deliver excellent customer service at a profit and to make United Bank of Philadelphia the "hometown" bank of choice. Our goal is to foster community development by providing quality personalized comprehensive banking services to business and individuals in the Greater Philadelphia Region, with a special sensitivity to Blacks, Hispanics, Asians and women.

TYPE OF FINANCING OFFERED: United Bank of Philadelphia provides financing assistance through the U S Small Business Administration (SBA) 7(a) Loan Program for

- Working capital
- Equipment and inventory purchases
- Leasehold improvements
- Business acquisition
- Commercial real estate acquisition
- Business debt refinancing

PIDC Community Capital

Address: 1500 Market Street, Philadelphia, PA 19102,

Telephone: 215-496-8139

WORKING CAPITAL & EQUIPMENT LOAN

Supports small and midsize businesses and nonprofits that need term financing for working capital, equipment, or leasehold improvements to support their growth.

CAPITAL PROJECT LOAN

For businesses or non-profit organizations undertaking capital projects such as building acquisition, renovation, leasehold improvements or equipment that need additional subordinate financing to complete the project.

CONTRACT LINE OF CREDIT

Provides small, minority, women, and disabled-owned businesses a line of credit to fund contract-related working capital.

LOAN RANGES: Working Capital and Equipment Loan- $50,000 to $750,000

Capital Project Loan- Range from $50,000 to $750,000, and one full-time equivalent job must be created for every $35,000 lent. PIDC can fund up to 40% of total project costs.

Contract Line of Credit- Starting at $50,000-Financing will not exceed 90% of the dollar value of the contract(s) being financed.

COST OF FINANCING (FEES): Working Capital and Equipment Loan- Fees will vary with each transaction and generally include:

APPLICATION: $250-$1000 depending on loan size - nonrefundable fee, payable at time of application submission

ORIGINATION: 1.5% of the financing amount provided, payable upon acceptance of PIDC's commitment letter.

CLOSING: Approximately $500 - $3,750, depending on loan size (does not include third party costs such as appraisals, construction monitoring, and UCC filings). Fees are subject to change. Please confirm all transaction fees with PIDC prior to application.

Capital Project Loan- Fees will vary with each transaction and generally include:

APPLICATION: $250 - $1000 depending on loan size - nonrefundable fee, payable at time of application submission.

ORIGINATION: 1.5% of the financing amount provided, payable upon acceptance of PIDC's commitment letter.

CLOSING: Approximately $500-$3,750 depending on loan size (does not include third party costs such as appraisals, construction monitoring, and UCC filings). Fees are subject to change. Please confirm all transaction fees with PIDC prior to application.

Contract Line of credit-Fees will vary with each transaction and generally include:

APPLICATION FEE: $250 - $1000 depending on loan size - nonrefundable fee, payable at time of application submission.

ORIGINATION FEE: 1.5% of the line of credit amount, payable upon acceptance of PIDC's commitment letter.

LEGAL FEE: Ranges from $500 to a maximum of $2,500, depending on loan size (does not include third party costs such as appraisals or UCC filings). Fees are subject to change. Please confirm all transaction fees with PIDC prior to application.

Community First Fund

Address: 1301 N. 2nd Street, Philadelphia, PA 19122

Telephone: 267-236-7001

DESCRIPTION OF SERVICES: Community First Fund is a private, independent non-profit Community Development Financial Institution (CDFI) whose mission is to provide capital in places where it is not generally available. We seek to create positive change in a community by providing entrepreneurs with access to business development loans for projects that generate jobs, create affordable housing and help to revitalize communities.

TYPE OF FINANCING OFFERED: We provide financing to both start up and growth small businesses located within our market area. We focus on business loans for minorities, women, nonprofit organizations, community development, educational opportunity, access to food and healthcare resources, and affordable housing... all intended to help build healthy communities.

Our business loan products fall into two categories: Small Business Loans and Microenterprise Loans. The amount of loans to early stage and startup businesses will be considered on a case-by-case basis.

- Microenterprise Loans
- Small Business Loans
- COMMERCIAL REAL ESTATE LOANS

- AFFORDABLE & MARKET RATE HOUSING LOANS
- COMMUNITY DEVELOPMENT LOANS

Economic Opportunities Fund

Address: 2010 Chestnut Street, Philadelphia, PA 19103,

Telephone: 215-564-5500

Impact Loan Fund, Inc.

Address: 1952 East Allegheny Avenue, Philadelphia, PA 19134,

Telephone: 215-423-2944

Philadelphia Neighborhood Housing Services, Inc.

Address: 5234 Chestnut Street, Philadelphia, PA 19139,

Telephone: 215-476-4205

Reinvestment Fund, Inc.

Address: 1700 Market Street, Philadelphia, PA 19103,

Telephone: 215-574-5829

The 504 Company

Address: 1515 Market Street, Suite 1200, Philadelphia, PA 19102,

Telephone: 855-504-7366 Toll Free, 215-854-6315 Direct

LISC Philadelphia

Address: 718 Arch Street, Suite 500 South, Philadelphia, PA 19106,

Telephone: (215) 923-3801, Fax: (215) 923-3168

Email: info-phila@LISC.org

DESCRIPTION OF SERVICES: LISC Philadelphia is one of 31 local offices of Local Initiatives Support Corporation (LISC), a national nonprofit community development organization and CDFI. Overall, LISC has invested $18.6 billion in neighborhoods and rural communities across the United States.

TYPE OF FINANCING OFFERED: We provide loans, grants, and technical assistance to local organizations for projects and programs that strengthen neighborhoods of choice and opportunity. Our loans and equity investments finance affordable housing, mixed-use projects, supermarkets, cultural centers, schools, health centers, and other vital community enterprises. We offer capacity building services to our grantees, partners, and borrowers as they undertake real estate development activities and programs that improve life in communities.

The Merchants Fund

Address: 1528 Walnut Street, Philadelphia, PA 19102,

Telephone: 215-399-1339

Email: info@merchantsfund.org

DESCRIPTION OF SERVICES: The Merchants Fund is a Philadelphia charity established in 1854 to provide charitable gifts to businesspersons facing financial hardship. Our Mission is to provide financial assistance to current and past merchants in Philadelphia.

City of Philadelphia-Philadelphia Lending Network

Philadelphia Commerce Department

Address: 1515 Arch Street, Philadelphia, PA 19102

Telephone: 215-683-2000

Complete the Financing Request Form. This form allows network members to learn more about your funding needs.

- Online: Fill out and submit the online form.
- By email: Complete the application, then email it to loan.info@phila.gov.
- By fax: Complete the application and fax to (215) 683-2150.

DESCRIPTION OF SERVICES: The Philadelphia Business Lending Network simplifies the process of applying for business loans. This service provides access to nonprofit and for-profit lenders with one form. You must have a small business in Philadelphia or have plans to move or expand to the city to qualify.

Participating organizations:

- American Heritage Federal Credit Union
- BB&T Bank
- Beech Business Bank
- Citizens Bank
- Community First Fund
- Cooperative Business Assistance Corporation (CBAC)
- Credibility Capital
- Customers Bank
- DNB First Bank
- The Enterprise Center

- Entrepreneur Works
- Finanta
- First State Community Loan Fund
- Franklin Mint Federal Credit Union
- Free Loan Association of Germantown (FLAG)
- Fulton Bank
- Hebrew Free Loan Society
- Impact Services Corporation
- Interface Financial Group
- Kiva
- Liquid Capital
- M&T Bank
- The Merchants Fund
- Noah Bank
- North Philadelphia Financial Partnership
- Parke Bank
- Philadelphia Industrial Development Corporation (PIDC)
- Port Richmond Savings
- Prudent Lenders
- Reinvestment Fund
- Republic Bank
- Santander Bank
- Tompkins VIST Bank
- United Bank of Philadelphia
- Univest Bank and Trust Co.
- Uplift Solutions
- Urban Seeds
- Wells Fargo Bank
- West Philadelphia Financial Services Institution
- Women's Opportunity Resource Center (WORK)

TYPE OF FINANCING OFFERED: Small Business loans

COST OF FINANCING (FEES): There is no cost to apply.

World Trade Center of Greater Philadelphia (WTCGP)

Address: 1617 John F. Kenny Blvd, Suite 1690

Telephone: 215-586-4240 x117; 215-586-4240

Email: dfoote@wtcphila.org wtcphila.org

DESCRIPTION OF SERVICES: The World Trade Center of Greater Philadelphia (WTCGP) provides a world-class portfolio of international trade services and key global connections to help the region's companies succeed in global markets, expanding the economic growth of the region. Services include international trade (export/import) counseling; education and training; trade missions and shows; market research; business matchmaking; financial resources; import assistance & global procurement; Export Finance Initiative International Design & Engineering Consortium (IDEC); Advancing Technology Exports Program CEO's China Operations Club; Latin American Trade Development Program Pennsylvania International Trade Guide.

Temple University SBDC

Address: 1510 Cecil B. Moore Avenue - Beech Building, Suite 200, Philadelphia, PA 19121,

Telephone: 215-204-7282

Email: sbdc@temple.edu/www.temple.edu/edu

The Temple University Small Business Development Center (SBDC) is one of 18 SBDCs in Pennsylvania. Our Center is funded by the Small Business Administration, Department of Community & Economic Development, and Temple University & the Fox

School of Business. Our mission is to provide entrepreneurs with the knowledge needed to make informed business decisions.

DESCRIPTION OF SERVICES:

One on One Consulting – Start-up and existing businesses can receive free business guidance from an SBDC consultant paired based on expertise. In the previous program year, most Temple SBDC clients sought services in start-up assistance, legal issues, and government contracting.

Workshops and Business Courses – Our current roster of seminars includes the 10-week Entrepreneurial Success Workshop Series, the award-winning Construction Management Certificate Series, and our newly launched Temple Business Roundtable.

Business Incubator and Co-Working Spaces – We house startup businesses in a setting that encourages entrepreneurship.

Legal Clinic – TU SBDC offers clients free services from the Beasley School of Law of Temple University. Our clients can receive supplemental services including contract review and corporation formation expertise.

University of Pennsylvania SBDC
Address: 3819 Chestnut Street, Suite 100, Philadelphia, PA M19104-3171,

Telephone: 215-898-4861

Website: Whartonsbdc.wharton.upenn.edu

The Wharton Small Business Development Center (SBDC), a division of the Snider Research Center of Wharton Entrepreneurship, is one of 18 SBDCs in Pennsylvania. We provide business assistance to small businesses in the Greater

Philadelphia region. Thousands of small businesses and entrepreneurs have benefited from our support since our founding in 1980. We hope that you too will benefit from our services.

DESCRIPTION OF SERVICES:

The Wharton SBDC has three principal programs which serve most small businesses and students:

Through the Business Building Program, each year a team of MBA candidates and experienced professionals develop a customized program for each of approximately 500 entrepreneurs who are starting or growing a business. Anchoring on their business goals, entrepreneurs take advantage of workshops and individual consultations to achieve their near-term business goals, such as writing a business plan, financing a business, developing a cash flow-based plan to grow their business or developing a marketing plan based on discovering their customers' real willingness to purchase.

Through the Growth Consulting Program, approximately 60 undergraduate and MBA students, following a competitive application process, work with more than 65 client businesses to help CEOs overcome strategic challenges and propel their companies' growth. In exchange, the "student consultants" gain valuable experience and refine their analytical and leadership skills. The Growth Consulting Practice is led by the Wharton SBDC's experienced professional staff with the support of Wharton faculty, senior advisors, Client Services staff, and Partners.

Through SBDC-Developed Projects for Wharton Courses, the WSBDC leverages its deep relationships with regional CEOs to structure more than 35 projects each year for courses across the School, including Leadership and Teamwork and Consulting to

High-Growth Companies. Through these projects, Wharton faculty and teaching assistants guide teams of Wharton students in highly structured projects defined by their course objectives and designed to benefit local small businesses.

Women's Business Development Center (WBDC)

Address: 1315 Walnut Street, Suite 1116, Philadelphia, PA 19107

Telephone: 215-790-9232

Website: www.womensbdc.org

DESCRIPTION OF SERVICES:

The Women's Business Development Center (WBDC) is a 501(c)(3) nationally recognized leader in the field of women's economic development. The organization was founded in 1986 to provide programs and services to support and accelerate women's business ownership and strengthen the impact of women on the economy by creating jobs, fueling economic growth, and building strong communities.

The mission of the Women's Business Development Center (WBDC) is to support and accelerate business development and growth, targeting women and serving all diverse business owners, in order to strengthen their participation in, and impact on, the economy.

The WBDC serves clients from all walks of life with a focus on women, minorities, and veterans (majority from low to moderate income areas), providing:

• Capacity building to scale businesses to compete in the marketplace.

- Technical assistance and financial support to help clients develop, manage, and grow businesses.

- Business financial education, including debt/equity placement and direct lending

- Customized business development services and support for veterans, childcare entrepreneurs, Latinas, and high science entrepreneurs.

- Corporate and public sector procurement opportunities; and

- Women's Business Enterprise (WBE) certification.

Women's Business Center at Assets

Address: 100 S. Queen Street, Lancaster, PA 17603

Telephone: 717-393-6089 EXT. 227

Website:
http://assetspa.org/programs/womens-business-center/

DESCRIPTION OF SERVICES:

The 10-second explanation of who we are at the Women's Business Enterprise Center (WBEC) East is that we are an advocate for women business owners and entrepreneurs in Pennsylvania, Delaware and Southern New Jersey. We believe diversity promotes innovation, opens doors, and creates partnerships that fuel the economy. That is why we provide the most relied upon certification standard for women-owned businesses, as well as world-class entrepreneurial training and education – combined with powerful tools and networking opportunities – to help them succeed.

WBEC East offers a comprehensive menu to help start your business with training, counseling, and networking programs and services, such as Entrepreneurial Training and a Business Finance Program. Funding for many of our Start-Up programs comes from our partnership with the U.S. Small Business Administration's Office of Women Business Ownership.

As one of the 14 regional partner organizations of the Women's Business Enterprise National Council (WBENC), we facilitate WBENC Certification, which validates that a business is at least 51 percent owned, controlled, operated and managed by a woman or women. This world-class certification standard is accepted by more than 1,000 corporations representing America's most prestigious brands, in addition to many states, cities and government entities.

WBEC-East also provides educational, networking, procurement-related, and informational programs and services that foster growth and business opportunities between certified women's business enterprises (WBEs) and purchasing entities, including major corporations and government agencies.

WBEC-East assists corporations in creating and building world-class supplier diversity programs – allowing them to: create new contractor partnerships and supplier sources, drive competition between existing and potential vendors, promote innovation, and demonstrate their organization's interest in the economic growth of the local, regional, and national economy.

COST OF SERVICES:

Fees Vary based on courses etc. call for details.

The Business Center

Address: 7500 Germantown Avenue, Elders Hall, Suite 113, Philadelphia, PA 19119

Telephone: 215-247-2433

Website: www.thebizctr.com

DESCRIPTION OF SERVICES:

The Business Center (TBC) is a 501(c)(3) that provides education and business networking programs necessary to strengthen business formation necessary to improve Northwest Philadelphia's business ecosystem for the underserved. Our programs better position small businesses and startups to develop and vet their business concepts and further establish their reputations. We achieve our mission by two primary means:

• By teaching the basic business "ins and outs" of accessing capital, marketing and building a team, we help individuals of any age gain confidence in knowing they can execute the fundamentals and understand what it means to be fully capitalized.

• We offer networking opportunities, targeted at growing industry sectors, which our members find invaluable in growing their businesses.

As evidence of our success, more than 300 adults and youth complete TBC's entrepreneurship courses each year, with 25 percent of these participants seeking on-going consulting services from TBC.

Finanta

Address: 1301 N. 2nd Street, Philadelphia, PA 19122,

Telephone: 267-236-7001

DESCRIPTION OF SERVICES:

FINANTA aims to help entrepreneurs succeed in business and life through comprehensive support services known as technical assistance. FINANTA's lenders and technical assistance providers offer entrepreneur clients business support services, credit building help, business training, grant application assistance, and referrals to resources ranging from business insurance to childcare.

Philadelphia MBDA Business Center

Address: 4548 Market Street, Philadelphia, PA 19139,

Telephone: 215-895-4024

DESCRIPTION OF SERVICES:

Access to Capital and Financial Management

Our business advisors offer extensive experience in:

- Commercial lending, banking and utilizing SBA Loans
- Financial and general finance counseling
- Credit and risk analysis

- Securing working capital

- Preparing loan packages

Business Consulting

Our services include individualized strategic and business planning, staffing, organizational structure consulting, and general business advising.

Access to Contracts and Markets

MBDA business development specialists provide procurement assistance to help minority-owned firms do business with federal, state, and local governments as well as private corporations.

DVIRC

Address: 2905 Southampton Road, Philadelphia, Pennsylvania 19154

Telephone: 215-464-8550

Email: info@dvirc.org

DESCRIPTION OF SERVICES:

DVIRC is a regional economic development organization with a public purpose—to support the profitable growth of small and mid-sized U.S. manufacturers.

Our vision is to have the region's manufacturing companies recognized as among the most advanced and innovative manufacturing companies in the world.

Our mission is to strengthen regional manufacturing companies by helping them continuously improve their competitiveness and increase their profitable growth.

Women Opportunities Resource Center

Address: 2010 Chestnut Street, Philadelphia, PA 19103

Telephone: 215-564-5500 ; Fax: 215-564-0933

Email: info@worc-pa.com

DESCRIPTION OF SERVICES:

IMPACT BUSINESS PLAN COMPETITION

Eligibility Requirements:

The Impact Business Plan Competition is meant to benefit women owned businesses (51% owned and managed by a woman). The awards are made possible by a generous grant from Citi Bank and additional support from Independence Blue Cross. The award is $2,500 to the first-place business and $1,000 to a second-place business. The winner will also receive free business services that are valued at $1,500 that will help them get to the next level. To enter the competition, you must be a for-profit woman owned company and meet all the following guidelines:

1. Must be 18 years of age or older and a resident of Philadelphia (including surrounding counties), New Jersey or Delaware with a working email address

2. Have completed the WORC training program (Start Smart or SET) or equivalent business plan training course with one of the participating partners or agree to complete the WORC training program prior to receiving the award funds

3. Demonstrate financial need for the award funds and show how they will advance the business

4. Business must show legal registration and required licensing in the State of Pennsylvania, New Jersey or Delaware prior to receiving award funds

5. Business must have or established bank account that is held under the business name

*Please Note: Award funds will be distributed by check to the business name once all eligibility requirements are confirmed. All funds must be used to advance the business, personal use is not allowed.

Entry:

To enter the business plan competition, you need to submit:

1. Complete the application online AND mail in a completed business plan to: WORC, Impact 2010 Chestnut Street, Philadelphia, PA 19103 (all questions must be answered, and documents signed; Incomplete applications will not be considered)

2. Submit a typed, bound copy of the business plan that includes all the sections listed in the outline.

Judging Criteria:

We are looking for businesses that can show:

• A strong social or community impact as a part of the regular operations or culture of the business

• A business concept that has a clearly identified customer base and has proven their willingness to buy the products or services

- A business plan that clearly communicates how the business will work (operations & marketing) and how the business will make money and provide a living return (sales & financials)

Timeline: Dates to be determined

Wharton Small Business Center

Address: 3819 Chestnut Street, Suite 100, Philadelphia, PA M19104-3171,

Telephone: 215-898-4861

DESCRIPTION OF TRAINING SERVICES:

SBDC-Developed Projects for Wharton Courses, the WSBDC leverages its deep relationships with regional CEOs to structure more than 35 projects each year for courses across the School, including Leadership and Teamwork and Consulting to High-Growth Companies. Through these projects, Wharton faculty and teaching assistants guide teams of Wharton students in highly structured projects defined by their course objectives and designed to benefit local small businesses.

Goldman Sachs 10,000 Small Businesses

Community College of Philadelphia

Address: 1700 Spring Garden Street, Room M1-22B, Philadelphia, PA 19130

Telephone: 267-299-5907; 267-299-5806 fax

Email: jhaile@ccp.edu.

DESCRIPTION OF TRAINING SERVICES: Goldman Sachs 10,000 Small Businesses is a program for small businesses that links learning to action. Through the program, participants will gain practical skills in topics such as negotiation, marketing and employee management that can immediately be put into action. In addition, they will receive the tools and professional support to develop a strategic and customized growth plan that will take their business to the next level.

Inner City Capital Connections Philadelphia

Address: 56 Warren Street, Suite 300; Roxbury, MA 02119
Telephone: 617-238-1740; Fax: 617-238-3001

DESCRIPTION OF TRAINING SERVICES: The ICCC Program is divided into four modules designed to maximize the participant's experience and accommodate their busy schedules.

• Opening Seminar: Full-day in-person training seminar where top business professors present on critical business topics

• Webinar Series: Virtual learning sessions to complement and deepen the learnings from the Opening Seminar

• Individual Coaching: Individual coaching focused on creating and refining capital pitch and/or tackling general business challenges

• National Conference: Culminating conference bringing together participants from across the country to continue their learning, sharpen their capital pitch, and connect with a growing network of growth-minded entrepreneurs and capital providers.

Inner City Capital Connections (ICCC) is a tuition-free executive leadership training program designed by the Initiative for a

Competitive Inner City (ICIC) to help business owners in economically distressed areas build capacity for sustainable growth in revenue, profitability, and employment. It is the only program of its kind to provide three critical elements for sustainable growth:

- Capacity-building education

- One-on-one coaching

- Connections to capital and capital providers.

SCORE Mentors Philadelphia

Address: 105 N. 22ND STREET; PHILADELPHIA, PA, 19103

Telephone: 215- 231-9880; FAX:(215) 231-9881

EMAIL: scorephila@yahoo.com

DESCRIPTION OF TRAINING SERVICES:

The Mission of the Philadelphia Chapter of SCORE is to continue the traditions started by our forefathers by growing small businesses by helping entrepreneurs and existing businesses solve problems through mentoring and support programs. Philadelphia is an all-volunteer organization and is funded through private sponsorship, corporate donations, and the City of Philadelphia, Department of Commerce.

Entrepreneur Works

Address: 400Market Street, Suite 210 ; Philadelphia, PA 19106

Telephone: 215-543-3100

Website: www.myentrepreneurworks.org

DESCRIPTION OF TRAINING SERVICES:

Classes

We offer multi-week business skills courses several times each year at our Philadelphia and Chester office locations. The Start It. Grow It. course aims to improve business performance by teaching practical considerations for starting a new business including defining a target market, pricing and business legal structures. The course has a flexible learning model and an emphasis on "learning by doing."

Workshops

We also offer a range of one-time workshops. Past topics have included "Getting my Idea to Fly," credit building, digital marketing, social media, alternate sources of financing, patents, and copywriting.

Women Business Development Center,

Address: 1315 Walnut Street Suite 1116; Philadelphia, Pennsylvania 19107
Telephone: 215-790-5059

Email: smerry@womensbdc.org

Website: http://www.womensbdc.org

DESCRIPTION OF TRAINING SERVICES:

The Women's Business Development Center - Philadelphia provides business training, counseling and other resources to help women in the Philadelphia area start and grow successful businesses. It is a member of the U.S. Small Business Administration's network of Women's Business Centers. Through management and technical assistance provided by entrepreneurs and counselors, the women's business centers offer women comprehensive training and counseling on a vast array of topics to help them start and grow their own businesses.

Women Opportunities Resource Center

Address: 2010 Chestnut Street; Philadelphia, PA 19103

Telephone: 215-564-0933-5500; Fax: 215-564-0933

Email: info@worc-pa.com

DESCRIPTION OF TRAINING SERVICES:

CREDIT REPAIR/CREDIT COUNSELING

The Women's Opportunities Resource Center (WORC) has partnered with CLARIFI to assist you with credit repair and credit counseling. This program is for those who want to learn more about their credit profile and clean up and re-establish their credit. The program teaches participants more about credit scores, how to improve them, and how to tell if there is inaccurate information on their profile.

One-on-One Counseling:

• Budget and Credit Counseling: Prepare analysis of income, living expenses and debt. Create a plan of action to avoid or reduce debt or reach other financial goals.

• Debt Management Counseling: Work with clients to eliminate or reduce debt. Work with creditors to lower payments, stop collection action and reduce/eliminate fees. Enroll in plan to make monthly payments to creditors via CLARIFI

- Credit Report Counseling: Help clients better understand their credit report and score. Review combined score and credit reports from three major credit reporting agencies. Develop an action plan to improve creditworthiness and/or maintain good credit.

- Housing Counseling (CLARIFI is certified by the U.S. Department of Housing and Urban Development (HUD) as a comprehensive housing counseling agency and also approved as a PA and NJ Housing Finance Agency.): Pre-Purchase, Foreclosure Prevention and Mortgage Default, Reverse Mortgage (Seniors 62 and older are eligible).

- Pre-Filing Bankruptcy Counseling (Clarify is approved to issue certificates evidencing completion of a pre-filing counseling session in compliance with the Bankruptcy Code. Approval does not endorse or assure the quality of a provider's services.): Review options and consequences for alternatives to bankruptcy. Review client's income, expenses, and budget.

SELF-EMPLOYMENT TRAINING PROGRAM

Provides individuals that have a business idea and possess transferable skills, or owners of existing part-time businesses, or those with fewer than 12 months of business operations the opportunity to take their business to the next level. The Start Smart business model employs next level marketing and formal business structures incorporated into a highly developed written business plan. Successful graduates will have developed and implemented legal business operations and are invited to participate in the WORC micro-loan program.

- Six-week program, meets two times per week (evenings)

- Covers business plan development, marketing, management and financing for Start-up and existing businesses. Consult with an Attorney, Accountant, and Other Professionals

- Successful participants will have completed a business plan, met all the local, state and federal requirements and be participating in actual business operations

- Helps participants evaluate, refine and develop their "micro" business by preparing a written business plan, including sections on marketing, operations and financials

- Qualifications: Open to all applicants

- Apply for WORC loan funds

COST OF TRAINING SERVICES:

Credit Repair and Counseling-No Fee

Self-Employment Training Program- Entrepreneurship Training Special only $175 ($99 for Low-Income). Regular Price is $350

Women Business Enterprise Center

Address: Philadelphia Building ; 1315 Walnut Street, Suite 1116, Philadelphia, PA 19107

Telephone: 215-790-9232

Website: www.womensbdc.org

DESCRIPTION OF TRAINING SERVICES:

The 10-second explanation of who we are at the Women's Business Enterprise Center (WBEC) East is that we are an advocate for women business owners and entrepreneurs in Pennsylvania, Delaware and Southern New Jersey. We believe diversity promotes innovation, opens doors, and creates partnerships that fuel the economy. That is why we provide the most relied upon certification standard for women-owned businesses, as well as world-class entrepreneurial training and education – combined with powerful tools and networking opportunities – to help them succeed.

WBEC-East began in 1995 as a Women's Business Center supported by the U.S. Small Business Administration. Since then, we have been working with small business owners throughout the Pittsburgh and Philadelphia areas, including Delaware and South Jersey to support women starting and growing their businesses. For the past two decades, we have been helping women achieve economic empowerment through entrepreneurship training courses. While the Center is dedicated to the economic empowerment of women, the services are open to all individuals.

Power UP, Community College of Philadelphia

Address: 1700 Spring Garden Street; Philadelphia. PA 19130

Telephone: 215- 496-6151

DESCRIPTION OF TRAINING SERVICES:

Power Up Your Business is a FREE, neighborhood-based approach to support small business owners in Philadelphia—like you—to give you the tools you need to grow your business and help your community thrive.

This new and innovative program was designed for businesses across Philadelphia. We are bringing entrepreneurs and business owners together to learn from one another, as we provide the education and training to help you adapt to challenges and run your business efficiently.

Community College of Philadelphia has a strong history of helping small businesses. In the past three years alone, we have helped nearly 300 small businesses grow their revenue and jobs, and we have provided counseling and resources to another 140 businesses in the past year.

Power Up offers the following:

- Store Owners Series
- Peer Based Learning Experience

Montgomery County

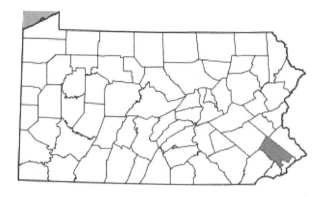

Montgomery County is the third-most populous county in the Commonwealth of Pennsylvania, and the 73rd-most populous in the United States. As of 2019, the census-estimated population of the county was 830,915, representing a 3.9% increase from the 799,884 residents enumerated in the 2010 census. Montgomery County is located adjacent to and northwest of Philadelphia. The county seat and largest city is Norristown. Montgomery County is geographically diverse, ranging from farms and open land in the extreme north of the county to densely populated suburban neighborhoods in the southern and central portions of the county.

Montgomery County is included in the Philadelphia-Camden-Wilmington PA-NJ-DE-MD metropolitan statistical area, sometimes expansively known as the Delaware Valley. The county marks part of the Delaware Valley's northern border with the Lehigh Valley region of Pennsylvania. In 2010, Montgomery County was the 51st-wealthiest county in the country by median household income. In 2008, the county was named the 9th Best Place to Raise a Family by Forbes.

Montgomery County is home to large and growing African American, Korean American, Puerto-Rican American, Mexican American, and Indian American populations. The county has the second-largest foreign-born population in the region, after Philadelphia County.

The median income for a household in the county was $60,829, and for a family was $72,183 (these figures had risen to $73,701 and $89,219, respectively, as of a 2007 estimate). Males had a median income of $48,698 versus $35,089 for females. The per capita income for the county was $30,898. About 2.80% of families and 4.40% of the population were below the poverty line, including 4.60% of those under age 18 and 5.10% of those age 65 or over.

Montco is also a major employment center with large business parks in Blue Bell, Lansdale, Fort Washington, Horsham, and King of Prussia which attract thousands of workers from all over the region. The strong job base and taxes generated by those jobs have resulted in Montgomery County receiving the highest credit rating of 'AAA' from Standard & Poor's, one of fewer than 30 counties in the United States with such a rating. In 2012, Moody's downgraded the general obligation rating to Aa1, and in 2018 the rating was revised back to Aaa.

Pennsylvania Assistive Technology Foundation

Address: 1004 West 9th Avenue, King of Prussia, PA 19406,

Telephone: 484-674-0506

DESCRIPTION OF SERVICES:

Pennsylvania Assistive Technology Foundation (PATF) is a statewide, non-profit organization that helps individuals with disabilities and older Pennsylvanians acquire the assistive technology devices and services they want. PATF is a state and federally certified Community Development Financial Institution (CDFI) and is the Commonwealth's designated Alternative Financing Program (AFP) under the federal Assistive Technology Act. PATF is one of 42 AFPs and state financing entities in the U.S. and territories.

TYPE OF FINANCING OFFERED:

PATF can help people with disabilities and older Pennsylvanians get the assistive technology they need with the following programs:

- Low-interest and 0% interest financial loans
- Information and assistance about possible funding resources

LOAN RANGES:

Mini-Loans- $100 – $2,000*

Low-Interest Loans-$2,000 and up

TABASFUNDING

Address: 355 W. Lancaster Avenue, Building E, Suite 1, Haverford, PA 19041

Telephone: 610-896-2400 ; Fax: 610-896-6199

Email: lee@TABASFUNDING.com

DESCRIPTION OF SERVICES:

TABASFUNDING provides Venture Capital/Angel Funding for entrepreneurs to expand or to acquire their businesses. We do this in Pennsylvania, New Jersey, and Delaware. Funding is available in amounts of $100,000 to $750,000 or more, in the form of flexible loans, which do not require any amount of collateral coverage. We may be able to help you when the bank says no, or when the bank will not lend you all of what you need. A common use is "gap" funding, where you need to fill the gap between money that you need, and what you have.

TYPE OF FINANCING OFFERED:

WORKING CAPITAL LOANS

A working capital loan is primarily used for financing inventory and accounts receivable

EXPANSION / ACQUISITION LOANS

A business that is expanding or acquiring another business needs funding

VENTURE CAPITAL LOANS

Venture Capital funding is generally where money is advanced to finance early stage businesses with strong growth potential

PROFESSIONAL LOANS

We would consider a professional someone who has specific education and must be approved by a supervisory body. This includes doctors, lawyers, and others

FRANCHISE LOANS

The decision and terms of our loan making to franchisees is not driven by collateral coverage alone. We will take what collateral is available, but that is a secondary consideration

CHILD CARE CENTER LOANS

Child Care Centers are a particularly satisfying type of funding to provide. There is a "triple bottom line"

MANUFACTURING LOANS

There is a consensus that most of Americans would like again to see more product manufactured in the United States. Manufacturing is a complex business and [principals need to be totally on top of all aspects, including raw materials, labor, research and development, and efficiency. We have deep experience lending in the manufacturing sector

HOSPITALITY AND RESTAURANT LOANS

As most businesspeople know, things usually cost more than expected. Our loans often have an interest only period while the operation develops

CONSTRUCTION LOANS

Because construction loans are expensive to administer, most banks are uninterested in loaning on smaller jobs under $1 million. This is where a private investor like Tabas funding comes through for contractors

REAL ESTATE ACQUISITION AND REHAB LOANS; PURCHASE OF PRIVATELY HELD MORTGAGES AND LOANS

We provide funding for acquisition and rehab of real estate. Unlike mortgages, these loans are specifically designed to be short-term

MEZZANINE LOANS

Mezzanine loans would be most appropriate for businesses that have a growth potential in excess of the general economy

LOAN RANGES:

You may apply for $100,000 to $750,000 or more.

COST OF FINANCING (FEES):

Typically, we charge no fees. We will ask that you pay any legal or other fees to document the loan.

COLLATERAL REQUIREMENT:

Typically, we charge no fees. We will ask that you pay any legal or other fees to document the loan.

MINIMUM CREDIT SCORE CONSIDERATION:

Principal or Principals must have reasonably good personal credit even if not extensive and be willing to guarantee. Businesses must be current in their bank loans, and current in any taxes or current on any agreements to catch up on back taxes.

Montgomery County Development Corporation

Address: Human Services Center - 5th Floor Commerce, 1430 DeKalb Street, Norristown, PA 19401

Telephone: 610-272-5000

DESCRIPTION OF SERVICES:

The Montgomery County Development Corporation, MCDC, promotes the growth of business, industry, and civic welfare in Montgomery County and facilitates the exchange of information between and among business, industry, and governmental institutions.

TYPE OF FINANCING OFFERED:

Montgomery County Opportunity Loan Program (MCOLP)

The Montgomery County Commerce Department is the "one-stop" entity for businesses seeking economic and workforce development assistance in Montgomery County. The Commerce Department's flagship economic development program is the Montgomery County Opportunity Loan Program (MCOLP). A cooperative initiative of the County government, the Montgomery County Development Corporation (MCDC), and the Montgomery County Industrial Development Authority (IDA), the loan program offers fixed rate and term loans to help businesses grow, increase productivity, and maximize the value of their investments in Montgomery County, Pennsylvania.

MCOLP is designed to be utilized as a traditional economic development "gap financing" tool in conjunction with commercial lenders as well as other public sector and non-profit sector lenders. Successful applicants will work with the MCDC Department staff and their financial institution(s) to fund a project (such as an equipment purchase or a building expansion). The advantages of utilizing MCOLP funding as part of a project's funding include a reasonable fixed rate and term.

LOAN RANGES:

Montgomery County Opportunity Loan Program- The maximum amount an Applicant can request when applying for MCOLP funding is the lesser amount of $250,000 or 50% of eligible project costs. Funding may be approved, at the discretion of the

Joint Loan Review Committee and/or the funding entities, at an amount less than what is requested.

COST OF FINANCING (FEES):

Montgomery County Opportunity Loan Program- The following is the fee schedule for applying to the MCOLP as of January 1, 2018:

• Pre-Application – No costs to the applicant.

• Application – Non-refundable $1,000 fee due at the time of application submission. The application review process will not commence until the application fee is paid in full.

• Closing Fee – One percent (1%) of the value of the loan due at the time of the loan closing.

In addition to the above fees, the Applicant Entity/Borrower shall pay all costs related to the filing of documents for collateralization, all costs related to the due diligence process during the Application review, and/or unanticipated out-of-pocket expenses of loan portfolio administration relating to the loan, including the fees and expenses of the servicers legal and other professional costs. The loan will not be considered satisfied and liens on collateral will not be released until such time as all fees and costs are paid in full.

Montgomery County Industrial Development Authority

Address: Human Services Center, 1430 DeKalb Street, 5th Floor, Norristown, PA 19401

Telephone: 610-278-3000

Email: MCIDA@montcopa.org

DESCRIPTION OF SERVICES:

The Industrial Development Authority (IDA) has assisted manufacturing firms, nonprofit (501(c)(3)) organizations, educational institutions and health care organizations, as well as water treatment plants and pollution control facilities. The IDA aims to maintain a high level of employment and create and maintain business opportunities.

TYPE OF FINANCING OFFERED:

HOW THE IDA WORKS

1. Borrowing money from private sector financing institutions

2. Loaning this money to Montgomery County companies to finance projects

3. Securing below-market interest rates on loans that are tax-exempt to the lender

Montgomery County SCORE

Address: Montgomery County Community College Center for Entrepreneurial Studies, Room 91, Parkhouse Hall' 340 DeKalb Pike, Blue Bell, PA 19406

Telephone: 215-885-3027

Website: www.montgomerycountypa.score.org

Pennsylvania Assistive Technology Foundation

Address: 1004 West 9th Avenue' King of Prussia, PA 19406

Telephone: 484-674-0506

DESCRIPTION OF TRAINING SERVICES:

As part of our financial education mission, we developed a book called Cents and Sensibility: A Guide to Money Management. Our pilot programs that used this book as a teaching manual taught us that all people, including those without disabilities, can benefit from this information. Everyone needs to understand how to manage their money so that their money does not manage them!

The Cents and Sensibility Educator Companion Manual was developed by a team of educators to accompany award-winning Cents and Sensibility: a guide to money management with accommodations for classroom use. While we strongly believe all students should receive a high-quality financial education, we know students with disabilities have unique financial education needs. This manual helps teachers develop relevant lessons and activities for students with and without disabilities on topics such as earning income, saving, and using financial services.

Delaware County

1By David Benbennick - The maps use data from nationalatlas.gov, specifically countyp020.tar.gz on the Raw Data Download page. The maps also use state outline data from statesp020.tar.gz.

Delaware County, colloquially referred to as Delco, is a county located in the U.S. state of Pennsylvania that borders Philadelphia. With a population of 566,747, it is the fifth most populous county in Pennsylvania, and the third smallest in area. The county was created on September 26, 1789, from part of Chester County, and named for the Delaware River.

Its county seat is Media. Until 1850, Chester was the county seat of Delaware County and, before that, of Chester County.

Delaware County is adjacent to the city-county of Philadelphia and is included in the Philadelphia–Camden–Wilmington, PA–NJ–DE–MD Metropolitan Statistical Area. Delaware County is the only county covered in its entirety by area codes 610 and 484.

Delaware County is roughly diamond- or kite-shaped, with the four sides formed by the Chester County boundary to the northwest, the boundary with the state of Delaware (a portion of the "Twelve Mile Circle") to the southwest, the Delaware River (forming the border with the state of New Jersey) to the southeast, and the city of Philadelphia and Montgomery County to the east and northeast.

The median income for a household in the county was $50,092, and the median income for a family was $61,590. Males had a median income of $44,155 versus $31,831 for females. The per capita income for the county was $25,040. About 5.80% of families and 8.00% of the population were below the poverty line, including 10.00% of those under age 18 and 7.10% of those age 65 or over.

Organizations

Chester Economic Development Authority

Address: One 4th Street, City Hall, P.O. Box 407, Chester, PA 19016-0407

Telephone: 610 447-7850, Fax 610 447-7856

DESCRIPTION OF SERVICES:

The Chester Economic Development Authority (CEDA) administers the Chester Small Business Loan Program to assist existing and start-up small businesses in expanding their operations and creating economic opportunities for low to moderate income persons.

TYPE OF FINANCING OFFERED:

SMALL BUSINESS LOANS

The Chester Economic Development Authority (CEDA) administers the Chester Small Business Loan Program to assist existing and start-up small businesses in expanding their operations and creating economic opportunities for low to moderate income persons.

ENTERPRISE ZONE REVOLVING LOAN FUND

The Chester Economic Development Authority also administers a Revolving Loan Fund Program for Enterprise Zone businesses. The purpose of the program is to assist in business growth and development that creates and retains jobs within the Enterprise Zone of the City of Chester.

LOAN RANGES:

Small Business Loan Fund- $30,000 to $30,000

Enterprise Zone Revolving Loan Fund_ $30,000 to $300,000

COST OF FINANCING (FEES):

Small Business Loans- loan program are as follows:

- Loan Application Fee $100.00

- Loan Commitment Fee 1%

- Attorney Fees Cost

- Filing Fees Cost

Enterprise Zone Revolving Loan Fund- Fees for the EZRLF loan program are as follows:

- Loan Application Fee $100.00

- Loan Commitment Fee 1%

- Attorney Fees Cost

• Filing Fees Cost

COLLATERAL REQUIREMENT:

Small Business Loan Fund- loans will be secured by appropriate levels of collateral. These may include notes, mortgages, personal guarantees, security agreements, assignment of contract revenues, etc. Collateral will be sufficient to recapture one hundred percent (100%) of the loan if default occurs.

Enterprise Zone Revolving Loan Fund- EZRLF loans will be secured by appropriate levels of collateral. These may include notes, mortgages, personal guarantees, security agreements, assignment of contract revenues, etc. Collateral will be sufficient to recapture one hundred percent (100%) of the loan if default occurs.

Delaware county SCORE
Address: Delaware County Chamber of Commerce, 1001 Baltimore Pike, Suite 9LL, Springfield, PA 19064

Telephone: 610-565-3677

Widener University SBDC
Address: 1350 Edgemont Avenue, University Technology Park, Building 2, Suite 130, Chester, PA 19013

Telephone: 610-619-8490

Website: www.widenersbdc.org

Chester County

Figure 2By David Benbennick - The maps use data from nationalatlas.gov, specifically countyp020.tar.gz on the Raw Data Download page.

Chester County (Pennsylvania German: Tscheschter Kaundi), colloquially known as Chesco, is a county in the U.S. state of Pennsylvania. As of the 2010 census, the population was 498,886, increasing by 5.2% to a census-estimated 524,989 residents as of 2019.[2] The county seat is West Chester.[3] Chester County was one of the three original Pennsylvania counties created by William Penn in 1682. It was named for Chester, England.

Chester County is part of the Philadelphia-Camden-Wilmington, PA-NJ-DE-MD Metropolitan Statistical Area. Eastern Chester County is home to many communities that comprise part of the Main Line western suburbs outside of Philadelphia, while part of its southernmost portion is considered suburban Wilmington, along with southwest Delaware County.

The median income for a household in the county was $65,295, and the median income for a family was $76,916 (these figures had risen to $80,818 and $97,894 respectively as of a 2007 estimate). Males had a median income of $51,223 versus $34,854 for females. The per capita income for the county was $31,627. About 3.10% of families and 5.20% of the population were below the poverty line, including 5.10% of those under age 18 and 5.50% of those age 65 or over.

Long a primarily rural area, Chester County is now the fastest-growing county in the Delaware Valley; it is one of the fastest growing in the entire Northeastern section of the United States.

Organizations

Seedcopa

Address: 737 Constitution Drive, Exton, PA 19341

Telephone: 610-321-8241

DESCRIPTION OF SERVICES:

We provide loans, grants, and technical assistance to local organizations for projects and programs that strengthen neighborhoods of choice and opportunity. Our loans and equity investments finance affordable housing, mixed-use projects, supermarkets, cultural centers, schools, health centers, and other vital community enterprises. We offer capacity building services to our grantees, partners, and borrowers as they undertake real estate development activities and programs that improve life in communities.

TYPE OF FINANCING OFFERED:

SEDCO provides financing for SBA 504 LOANS AND SBA 7A loans

SBA 504: The Small Business Administration (SBA) 504 loan is part of a government small business program to help put your own business goals within reach. The SBA is a U.S. government body, with the motive of providing support for small businesses and entrepreneurs. For each loan authorized, a government-backed guarantee offers serious credibility, since the lender knows that even if you default, the government will pay off the balance. The 504 loan offers a fixed-rate and long-term financing. These loans are great for applicants whose business model will benefit their community directly, either by providing jobs or bringing needed services to an underserved area. For many small businesses, it is beneficial because this is money and capital that may not be accessible through traditional loans.

SBA 7A: The Small Business Administration (SBA) 7A loan is designed to finance an existing array of small business needs. The SBA is a U.S. government body, with the motive of providing support for small businesses and entrepreneurs. For each loan authorized, a government-backed guarantee offers serious credibility, since the lender knows that even if you default, the government will pay off most of the balance. The 7(a) Loan Program is SBA's primary program for helping start-up and existing small businesses, with financing guaranteed for a variety of general business purposes. For many small businesses, it is beneficial because this is money and capital that may not be accessible through traditional loans.

Businesses may use the 7a loan for the following:

- Purchase commercial real estate

- Pay for machinery and equipment

- Buy an existing business

- Fund leasehold improvements

- Finance start-up business

- Acquire inventory

- Provide permanent working capital

LOAN RANGES:

SBA 7(A): UP TO $5 MILLION

SBA 504: Up to $12 million

Chester County Economic Development Council

Address: 737 Constitution Drive, Exton, PA 19341

Telephone: 610.344-6910

Website: www.chescodelscore.org

DESCRIPTION OF SERVICES:

The CCEDC is a private, non-profit, economic development organization promoting smart growth in Chester County and the surrounding region for over 50 years.

Through collaboration with public and private sectors, we initiate, implement and innovate programs that improve the business climate and community, making Chester County, PA a premier location to live and work.

SCORE Chester

Address: 601 WESTTOWN ROAD #281, West Chester, PA, 19380

Telephone: 610 344-6910; Fax: 610 344-6919

Email: help@score.org

DESCRIPTION OF SERVICES:

Our business professionals offer free mentoring that will help your business succeed. SCORE has been mentoring new and existing businesses for over forty years. Each SCORE member is dedicated to delivering, valuable, timely and practical business advice. There is no charge for mentoring, no matter how many sessions are needed.

SCORE provides an extensive variety of regularly scheduled low cost business workshops and seminars. From basic sessions on how to start and grow a business to hands on financial exercises, all workshops and seminars are designed to help you establish and grow a successful business.

COST OF SERVICES: Free

Chester County Economic Development Council

Address: Eagleview Corporate Center, 737 Constitution Drive, Exton, PA 19341

Telephone: 610.344-6910

Website: www.chescodelscore.org

DESCRIPTION OF TRAINING SERVICES:

Educating and Engaging Workers and Youth for Future Opportunities

The success of any business or organization lies in its human capital. Finding and developing our human capital is especially critical in this global economy. CCEDC creates human capital by addressing the workforce and economic development needs of industry partners in the region.

Collaborating with the Chester County Workforce Development Board and numerous strategic organizations, CCEDC developed and implemented five Industry Partnerships (IPs) to serve businesses in Chester County and the region. IPs bring together business, education, economic development and industry associations, around the common purpose of improving the competitiveness of a cluster of companies, focusing primarily on their workforces. The IPs leverage the resources of the partnership to help address common industry challenges such as developing human capital, accessing business financing and resources, and developing innovative responses to emerging business trends and opportunities.

Workforce Development spans the spectrum of training and education options. CCEDC with its partners provide:

• Career Exploration Initiatives for K-12 students and business experiences for college students serve over 2,000 students annually: and

• Incumbent Worker Training is offered for employees in more than 500 of our area's companies; and

• Rebranding and Re-employment Support for job seekers in transition through the Hire One Initiative and CareerLink.

Bucks County

3By David Benbennick - The maps use data from nationalatlas.gov, specifically countyp020.tar.gz on the Raw Data Download page.

Bucks County is a county located in the Commonwealth of Pennsylvania. As of the 2010 census, the population was 625,249, making it the fourth-most populous county in Pennsylvania and the 99th-most populous county in the United States. The county seat is Doylestown. The county is named after the English county of Buckinghamshire or more precisely, its abbreviation.

Bucks County constitutes part of the northern boundary of the Philadelphia–Camden–Wilmington, PA–NJ–DE–MD Metropolitan Statistical Area, more commonly known as the Delaware Valley. It is located immediately northeast of Philadelphia and forms part of the southern tip of the eastern state border with New Jersey.

The boroughs of Bristol and Morrisville were prominent industrial centers along the Northeast Corridor during World War II. Suburban development accelerated in Lower Bucks in the 1950s with the opening of Levittown, Pennsylvania, the second such "Levittown" designed by William Levitt.

Among Bucks' largest employers in the twentieth century were U.S. Steel in Falls Township, and the Vulcanized Rubber & Plastics and Robertson Tile companies in Morrisville. Rohm and Haas continue to operate several chemical plants around Bristol. Waste Management operates a landfill in Tullytown that is the largest receptacle of out-of-state waste in the USA (receiving much of New York City's waste following the closure of Fresh Kills landfill in Staten Island, NY 40 miles (64 km) away).

Bucks is also experiencing rapid growth in biotechnology, along with neighboring Montgomery County. The Greater Philadelphia area consistently ranks in the top 10 geographic clusters for biotechnology and biopharma.[11] It is projected by 2020 that one out of four people in Bucks County will work in biotechnology.

Organizations

Bucks County Economic Development Corporation

Address: 115 West Court Street, Second Floor, Doylestown, PA 18901

Telephone: 215-348-9031;Fax: 215-348-8829

DESCRIPTION OF SERVICES:

Bucks County Economic Development Corporation (BCEDC) is a non-profit, non-political economic development organization established in 1958 to support economic growth in Bucks County. BCEDC is a Commonwealth of Pennsylvania certified economic development agency. BCEDC offers low cost financing options for land/building, machinery and equipment. These and other incentive programs offered through BCEDC create a strong and vital economy for Bucks County and in return create and retain jobs for Bucks County residents.

TYPE OF FINANCING OFFERED:

Business Builder Loan Fund (BBLF)

The Bucks County Economic Development Corporation Business Builder Loan Program was established to provide funding to small and emerging Bucks County companies.

Pennsylvania Industrial Development Authority (PIDA)

Job Creation or Job Retention Program

The purpose of PIDA is to stimulate the construction of industrial buildings and/or development projects to increase employment in Pennsylvania with the focus on job creation or job retention.

Diverse Business Financing Initiative (DBFI)

The Pennsylvania Department of Community and Economic Development has launched the Diverse Business Financing Initiative (DBFI) to support and grow qualifying diverse businesses committed to full-time job creation and retention. Certified small businesses operated by minorities, women, veterans, service-disabled veterans, LGBT individuals, and more qualify for low-interest loans packaged and underwritten by the Bucks County Economic Development Corporation (BCEDC) in partnership with PIDA.

Revenue Bond and Mortgage Program (RBM)

(Industrial Revenue Bonds - Tax-exempt of Taxable)

The Revenue Bond and Mortgage Program is a financing program provided by the Commonwealth to stimulate economic development and create jobs. This objective is attained by providing tax-free, low interest loans to business and industry. One job must be retained or created for each $50,000 borrowed through the Revenue Bond and Mortgage Program.

LOAN RANGES:

Diverse Business Financing Initiative- The BCEDC will provide loans up to $100,000 to businesses that receive certification from third-party organizations and are operated by:

- minorities - women - veterans - service-disabled veterans - disabled individuals - LGBT individuals

Revenue Bond and Mortgage Program- The maximum capital expenditure allowed on a project in the period of three years prior to and three years after the project date is $20,000,000.00. If that limit is exceeded, the bond or mortgage issue becomes taxable retroactively.

COST OF FINANCING (FEES):

Business Builder Loan Fund- Each application must be accompanied by a $1000 non-refundable application fee. A 1% placement fee will be charged at closing in addition to legal fees including document preparation and processing.

Pennsylvania Industrial Development Authority- Charges by Bucks County Economic Development Corporation include a non-refundable $2,000 application fee as well as a 1% of the project loan amount due at the time of signing the PIDA commitment letter. One percent of the PIDA loan is charged (minimum $500) by PIDA when their commitment letter is accepted. Other costs include legal and bank fees (if a bank is involved in the project).

Revenue Bond and Mortgage Program- Fees charged by Industrial Development Authority include a non-refundable $2,000.00 application fee, a 1% placement fee at the time of closing, Industrial Development Authority legal fees as well as any bank fees.

COLLATERAL REQUIREMENT:

Diverse Business Financing Initiative- Collateral is required based on the asset being financed. A variety of factors are considered, including mortgages, machinery and equipment, inventory, and receivables.

The interest rate and collateral are to be negotiated upon approval of the initial loan application.

Bucks County Industrial Development Authority

Address: 11 Welden Drive - Suite 100, Doylestown, PA 18901

Telephone: 267 880-6071

Email: inquiries@buckscountyida.com

DESCRIPTION OF SERVICES:

The Bucks County Industrial Development Authority (BCIDA) was established in 1967 and since that time has been a leader in providing tax-free financing to hundreds of industrial and manufacturing enterprises that account for billions of dollars in new private investment and thousands of family sustaining jobs.

As the lead coordinator of economic development within the county, BCIDA has assisted in facilitating millions of dollars of

Pennsylvania Industrial Development Authority (PIDA) financing that is frequently part of a larger financing package. We have also worked closely with the county's Redevelopment Authority in the designation of redevelopment areas, the success of the state supported Enterprise Zone Program, and in the successful redevelopment of Brownfield sites throughout the county. Currently, the BCIDA manages nearly $10 million in federal and local loan funds.

TYPE OF FINANCING OFFERED:

The Bucks County Industrial Development Authority's Industrial Revenue Bond and Mortgage Program can provide capital financing for manufacturing companies such as exempt facilities and non- profit organizations. This can be achieved either through tax free mortgages for smaller projects or a stand-alone bond issue for larger ones. Both approaches can significantly reduce borrowing costs.

The Revenue Bond and Mortgage program can prove an attractive mechanism for financing new business and related expansions. But the program is governed by federal statute, so it is important to work closely with an experienced and qualified team in order to ensure correct procedure is followed. Fortunately, the BCIDA has nearly 40 years' experience in raising hundreds of millions of dollars for qualified applicants through this program.

Core Industry Fund- Over $2 million is available in low interest financing to assist small businesses to grow and expand, particularly those seeking to acquire and improve blighted properties in distressed areas, areas of higher unemployment, or within Bucks County's state designated Enterprise Zone.

New Economy Fund- Over $2 million in discounted financing is available to assist the BCIDA in pursuing a policy of 'intelligent growth'

LOAN RANGES:

Revenue Bond and Mortgage Program-While there is no minimum size for tax-exempt mortgages or bonds, it is generally not economical to issue bonds for amounts under $1,000,000. Amounts under $1,000,000 can be funded through a tax-exempt mortgage. The maximum size for a manufacturing project is $10 million.

Core Industry Fund- Businesses can secure as much as $400,000 in funding from this program to support these kinds of ventures, so long as more than half the jobs created go to low and/or moderate income workers (generally a worker for whom no specialized skills are needed to perform the job for which they are hired or for underemployed or unemployed individuals), or the funds are used to prevent or eliminate blight (generally an area or building that cannot reasonably be occupied in its present state).

New Economy Fund- Businesses and investor/developers can secure as much as $500,000 in funding from this program to support these kinds of ventures, so long as there is at least a dollar for dollar match in debt and equity financing.

Upper Bucks County Technical School

Address: 3115 Ridge Road, Perkasie, PA 18944

Telephone: 215-795-2011

Email: eevans@ubtech.org ubtech.org

DESCRIPTION OF SERVICES:

Upper Bucks County Technical School (UBCTS) is a regional career and technology center offering career training in 21 different program areas. Advanced Manufacturing training programs include Mechatronics, Precision Machining, and Welding & Fabrication. UBCTS serves approximately 700 high school students during the day, but on evenings and weekends, we offer technical skill training to adults. When you need technical skills training, think UBCTS! Conveniently located in the Upper Bucks region, we offer modern, state of the art manufacturing labs, apprenticeship training, and industry experienced   instructors. Partner with us so we can help you find your next employee or student intern, train your current employees in our adult education classes, and/ or provide customized, targeted training to meet your specific needs.

Strategic Early Warning Network (SEWN)

Buck County Economic Development Corporation

Address: 115 West Court Street, Second Floor, Doylestown, PA 18901

Telephone: 215-348-9031

Email: sewnse@steelvalley.org

DESCRIPTION OF SERVICES:

SEWN is Pennsylvania state funded program targeting stressed manufacturing organizations. A stressed organization is defined as one in danger of eliminating jobs should negative business trends continue. The services of this program are offered to these businesses free of charge. The SEWN turnaround consultant works in   conjunction with other state funded partners.

Services include financial: restore cash flow, working capital and re-financing of debt; sales and marketing: including new plans, new customers and markets; revised business strategy; ownership transition; operations and technology improvement. Serving Bucks, Berks, Chester, Delaware, Montgomery and Philadelphia Counties.

COST OF SERVICES:

Free of Charge

Delaware Valley Industrial Resource Center (DVIRC)

Address: 2905 Southampton Road, Suite B, Philadelphia, PA 19154

Telephone: 215-464-8550

Email: rcrossett@dvirc.org dvirc.org

DESCRIPTION OF SERVICES:

DVIRC is an Economic Development organization committed to assisting small and medium-sized manufacturing enterprises compete and grow in the global economy. For nearly 25 years we have provided best practice services to address the strategic and operational needs of advanced manufacturers, in every industry sector. Our experienced professionals come from industry & work closely with manufacturing leaders and their teams. We provide: • Continuous Improvement (CI) /Lean Enterprise • Strategy, Sales & Marketing • Supply Chain Optimization /Quality Certifications HR for Hire / Training • Executive Network Groups

Lower Bucks County Chamber of Commerce

Address: 409 Hood Boulevard Fairless Hills, PA 19030

Telephone: 215-943-8850

Website: score570@verizon.net / buckscounty.score.org

DESCRIPTION OF SERVICES:

Bucks County SCORE provides business mentoring and training to entrepreneurs and small business owners. Whether you are just thinking about owning your own business or are looking to grow your existing business, we offer no-cost, high value one-on-one mentoring sessions with certified business professionals, and free or low-cost training through online and in-class educational workshops. We have counseled businesses in many industries, including retail, food services, import/export, non-profit, technology, and more. Our counseling sessions and educational workshops cover such topics as: business planning; funding sources; marketing and social media; sales; accounting and finance; operations; patents and trademarks.

Bucks County SCORE
Address: 11 Welden Drive, Doylestown, PA 18901

Telephone: 215-943-8850

Website: www. buckcounty.score.org

Bucks County Workforce Development Board (BCWDB) & PA CareerLink® Bucks County

Address: 1268 Veterans Hwy, Bristol, PA 19007

Telephone: 215-781-1073 x 2203; 215-874-2800

Email: jpeterson@buckscareerlink.org

DESCRIPTION OF TRAINING SERVICES:

The Bucks County Workforce Development Board (BCWDB) is a non-profit organization, serving as the fiscal agent for federal and state workforce funds allocated to Bucks County. The BCWDB continuously strives to increase and improve its stewarding and investing of public workforce dollars. The BCWDB works to ensure that the Bucks County workforce system, covering numerous agencies and multiple disciplines via the Pennsylvania CareerLink® Bucks County, meets both employers' needs for skilled workers and workers' needs for career and economic advancement. The BCWDB oversees the development of partnerships with employers, economic development and educational agencies, and other programs to leverage available resources for the benefit of our local workforce.

Bucks County Community College

Address: 275 Swamp Road, Newtown, PA 18940

Telephone: 215-968-8364

Email: susan.herring@bucks.edu

DESCRIPTION OF TRAINING SERVICES:

Bucks County Community College's Center for Workforce Development provides high value customized training for businesses to help them grow and prosper by up skilling incumbent workers. Topics include leadership and supervision, human resources, computer applications, professional business communications and more. Our instructors are industry professionals who understand your challenges in today's business world, and how to maximize time and results for your learners. We deliver at all three of our campuses or on site at your business. We administer WEDnetPA grant funds to help defray the cost of training for a variety of industries. We also offer industrial skills training at our Advanced Manufacturing Training Center, much of it grant funded by grants from the County and State.

Lancaster County

Lancaster County locally /ˈlæŋkəstər/, (Pennsylvania German: Lengeschder Kaundi) sometimes nicknamed the Garden Spot of America or Pennsylvania Dutch Country, is a county located in the south-central part of the Commonwealth of Pennsylvania. As of the 2010 census, the population was 519,445. Its county seat is Lancaster.

Lancaster County comprises the Lancaster, Pennsylvania, Metropolitan Statistical Area.

The County of Lancaster is a popular tourist destination, with its Amish community a major attraction.

In 2004, the county had a per capita personal income (PCPI) of $30,790, 93% of the national average. This reflects a growth of 4.5% from the prior year, versus a 5.0% growth for the nation as a whole. Despite the lower income, the county poverty rate in 2003 was 8.3% compared to a national rate of 12.5%. In 2004, federal spending in Lancaster County was $4,199 per resident, versus a national average of $7,232.

In 2005, Lancaster County was 10th of all counties in Pennsylvania with 17.7% of its workforce employed in manufacturing; the state averages 13.7%, and the leader, Crawford County, has only 25.1%.

Lancaster County lags in information workers, despite being the corporate headquarters of MapQuest. It ranks 31st in the state with 1.3% of the workforce; the state as a whole employs 2.1% in information technology.

The county ranks 11th in the state in managerial and financial workers, despite having 12.5% of the workforce in those occupations (versus the state average of 12.8%). The state leaders are Chester County with 20.5% and Montgomery County with 18.5%.

With 17.3% working in the professions, Lancaster County is 31st in Pennsylvania, compared to a state average of 21.5%. Centre County leads with 31.8%, undoubtedly due to Penn State's giant footprint in an otherwise rural county, but the upscale Philadelphia suburbs of Montgomery County give them 27.2%.

Lancaster County ranks even lower, 34th, in service workers, with 13.3% of the workforce, compared to a state average of 15.8%. Philadelphia County leads with 20.5%.

Lancaster County has an unemployment rate of 7.8% as of August 2010. This is a rise from a rate of 7.6% the previous year.

Organizations

Community First Fund

Address: 30 West Orange Street, P.O. Box 524, Lancaster, PA 17608-0524

Telephone: 717.393.2351

TYPE OF FINANCING OFFERED:

Installment loans, lines of credit and technical assistance for minority business enterprises, women-owned business enterprises and small businesses.

Lancaster Housing Opportunity Partnership

Address: 123 East King Street, Lancaster, PA 17602

Telephone: (717) 291-9945

DESCRIPTION OF SERVICES:

Founded in 1994 in Lancaster County, the Lancaster Housing Opportunity Partnership (LHOP) is a community benefit 501(c)(3) organization created by county and municipal government, business and civic leaders focused housing affordability for low to moderate income people. In July of 2015 LHOP became a U.S. Treasury certified Community Development Financial Institution (CDFI) serving Adams, Cumberland, Dauphin, Franklin, Lancaster, Lebanon, Perry & York Counties.

PA Department of Community & Economic Development Center for Private Financing Commonwealth

Address: Keystone Building 400 North Street, 4th Floor, Harrisburg, PA 17120-0225

Telephone: 717-783-1109

DESCRIPTION OF SERVICES:

The Business Opportunities Fund (BOF) was established in 2008. The purpose of this program is to assist small minority or woman-owned contractors and other small business owners who lack access to lines of credit or small business loans from traditional financial institutions. Lack of access to credit prevents these businesses from competing for governmental and private sector contracts. These business owners often require technical assistance in governmental procurement including achieving necessary certification and bid preparation. The BOF is designed to assist borrowers with both financing and technical assistance.

TYPE OF FINANCING OFFERED:

1. Cash flow (working capital): Including most business operation and expansion expenses.
2. Equipment: Includes acquisition, delivery, installation, and renovation of new and used equipment.
3. Leasehold improvements
4. Acquisition of owner-occupied commercial real estate

LOAN RANGES:

There are no minimum or maximum loan sizes.

Economic Development Company of Lancaster County & EDC Finance Corporation

Address: 115 East King Street, Lancaster, PA 17602

Telephone: 717.397.4046

DESCRIPTION OF SERVICES:

The Economic Development Company of Lancaster County (EDC) is the leading organization dedicated to promoting business development and expansion within Lancaster County, Pennsylvania. A private, not-for-profit, non-government organization, founded in 1960, EDC works on several fronts to promote the economic well-being of our communities. Whether you are starting up your business, expanding your presence here or considering a corporate relocation, EDC can assist you with everything from site location to financing.

TYPE OF FINANCING OFFERED:

Business Financing

EDC Finance is Lancaster County's business and production agriculture source for SBA 504, Pennsylvania Industrial Development Authority, Building PA, and IDA financing.

EDC Finance was designated the 2014 U.S. Small Business Administration Philadelphia District Office Certified Development Company of the Year. EDC Finance is your Certified Development Company for SBA 504 loans in Lancaster County and throughout South-Central PA, including official strategic alliances with our economic development partners in Adams, Cumberland, and York Counties.

EDC Finance assists companies across all industries with fixed asset financing for real estate and capital equipment projects. Prominent economic development lending tools through the Small Business Administration (SBA 504) and Pennsylvania Industrial Development Authority provide valuable long-term fixed interest rates...

EDC Finance understands the importance of production agriculture to our local economy and is proud to support several economic development financing tools available to assist with farm purchases, barn constructions, and related equipment. From dairy to hogs and broilers to layers, EDC Finance is experienced in agricultural economic...

EDC Finance offers financial support to Pennsylvania developers and their redevelopment and construction projects in Lancaster County and its urban districts. If you're building an industrial park or site accommodating single or multi-business tenants, you may qualify for one of EDC Finance's Developer Financing programs...

LOAN RANGES:

Small Business Fund-$400,000 maximum loan amount for all borrowers up to 50% of project costs

- Small Business Administration 504-
- $5 million maximum loan amount for most borrowers up to 40% of project costs
- $5.5 million maximum loan amount for manufactures & certain energy efficient projects up to 40% of project costs
- Real Estate Fund- $2,000,000 maximum loan amount for all borrowers up to 50% of project costs
- Community Development Fund-$200,000 maximum loan amount for all borrowers up to 50% of project costs

COST OF FINANCING (FEES):

Small Business Fund-

- 1.5% commitment fee (production agriculture fee is reduced by 0.50% to 1.00%)

- $2,500 – $3,000 attorney and recording costs

- Title insurance is required for real estate transactions

Small Business Administration 504-

- 0.5% participation fee based on senior loan amount (out-of-pocket)

- 2.2% commitment and underwriting fee (debenture funded)

- $3,000 attorney and recording costs (debenture funded)

- Title insurance is required for real estate transactions

Real Estate Fund-

- 1.5% commitment fee

- 1.0% PIDA approval & closing fee

- Title insurance is required

Community Development Fund-

- 1.5% commitment fee

- $500 recording costs

- Title insurance is required for real estate transactions

City of Lancaster

Address: 120 North Duck Street, P.O.Box 1599, Lancaster, PA 17608

Telephone: 717-291-4711

DESCRIPTION OF SERVICES:

The City of Lancaster has established a Small Business Loan Program to provide special rate financing to small businesses locating or expanding in the City of Lancaster. Loans will be made to stimulate business growth, job retention and job creation opportunities and to enhance the local community tax base. While the program is principally designed to provide gap financing to applicants, the City will consider being a primary lender for qualified small business start-ups and non-profit economic development projects.

TYPE OF FINANCING OFFERED:

The Small Business Loan Program will be made available to those businesses located or planning to locate within the City of Lancaster.

LOAN RANGES:

Micro Enterprise Loan (start-up business): The fixed asset financing and working capital up to 90% of the total financing needed; not to exceed $20,000. b. Enterprise Loan: Fixed asset financing up to 80% of the total financing needed; not to exceed $250,000. Working capital loans may be considered but limited to $20,000 for qualified applicants.

COST OF FINANCING (FEES):

The loan processing fee is 1% of the loan amount at the time of settlement. The borrower shall also pay all closing costs including the City's legal fees, up to $5,000. The exact fee shall be provided prior to closing

COLLATERAL REQUIREMENT:

Depending on the project and the financial status of the applicant, the following will be considered as suitable collateral:

a. Personal guarantees of all principals owning or controlling more than 20% of the business b. Personal guarantees of other individuals or parties subject to credit reports and confirmation of the assets being pledged c. Personal property of the applicant or immediate family members including homes, second homes, investment properties and stocks pledged to the City. Personal property not permitted is vehicles, boats, motorcycles, clothing, jewelry, etc. An escrow fund established and controlled by the City.

Wilmington, DE

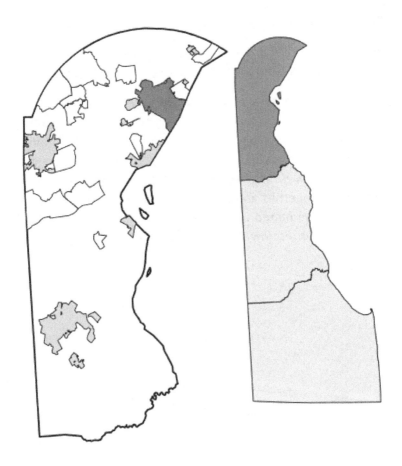

Wilmington (Lenape: Paxahakink / Pakehakink) is the largest and most populous city in the U.S. state of Delaware. The city was built on the site of Fort Christina, the first Swedish settlement in North America. It lies at the confluence of the Christina River and Brandywine River, near where the Christina flows into the Delaware River.

As of the census of 2010, there were 70,851 people, 28,615 households, and 15,398 families residing in the city. The population density was 6,497.6 per square mile (2,508.8/km2). There were 32,820 housing units at an average density of 3,009.9 per square mile (1,162.1/km2) and with an occupancy rate of 87.2%.

According to ACS 1-year estimates for 2010, the median income for a household in the city was $32,884, and the median income for a family was $37,352. Males working full-time had a median income of $41,878 versus $36,587 for females working full-time. The per capita income for the city was $24,861. 27.6% of the population and 24.9% of families were below the poverty line. 45.7% of those under the age of 18 and 16.5% of those 65 and older were living below the poverty line.

Much of Wilmington's economy is based on its status as the most populous and readily accessible city in Delaware, a state that made itself attractive to corporations with business-friendly financial laws and a longstanding reputation for a fair and effective judicial system. Contributing to the economic health of the downtown and Wilmington Riverfront regions has been the presence of Wilmington Station, through which 665,000 people passed in 2009.

Wilmington has become a national financial center for the credit card industry, largely due to regulations enacted by former Governor Pierre S. du Pont, IV in 1981. The Financial Center Development Act of 1981, among other things, eliminated the usury laws enacted by most states, thereby removing the cap on interest rates that banks may legally charge customers. Major credit card issuers such as Barclays Bank of Delaware (formerly Juniper Bank), are headquartered in Wilmington.

Organizations

First State Community Loan Fund

Address: 100 W. 10th Street, Suite 1005, Wilmington, DE 19801

Telephone: 302-652-6774

Website: www.firststateloan.org

Delaware Community Investment Corporation

Address: 100 West 10th Street, Suite 302, Community Service Building, Wilmington, DE 19801

Telephone: 302-655-1420

Eagle One Federal Credit Union

Address: 3301 Philadelphia Pike, Claymont, DE 19703

Telephone: 215 742-9611; 844 218-4529

TYPE OF FINANCING OFFERED:

- Commercial Mortgages

- Equipment/Vehicle Loans

- Business Credit Cards

- Payment Processing Services

- SBA Lending Programs

- Working Capital Lines of Credit

- Business Accounts

- USDA Guaranteed Lending

Delaware State Score

Address: The Nemours building, 1007 North Orange Street, Suite 1120, Wilmington, DE 19801

Telephone: 302-573-6552

Email: info@scoredelaware.org

Reading, PA

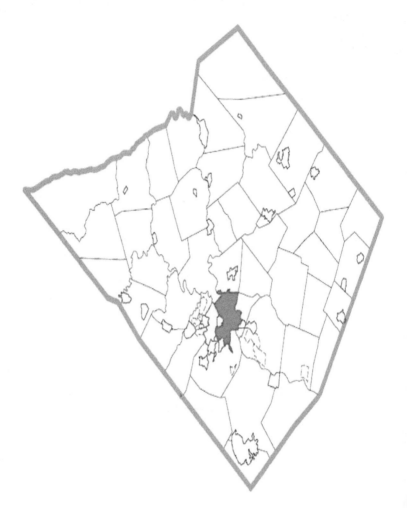

Reading (/ˈrɛdɪŋ/ RED-ing; Pennsylvania German: Reddin) is a city in and the county seat of Berks County, Pennsylvania, United States. With a population of 88,082 as of the 2010 census, it is the fifth-largest city in Pennsylvania. Located in the southeastern part of the state, it is the principal city of the Greater Reading Area, home to 420,152 residents, and is furthermore included in the greater Delaware Valley. According to the 2010 census, Reading had the highest share of citizens living in poverty in the nation for cities with populations of more than 65,000. Reading's poverty rate fell over the next decade. Reading's poverty rate in the 2018 five-year American Community survey showed that 35.4% of the city's residents were below the poverty line, or less "than the infamous 41.3% from 2011, when Reading was declared the poorest small city in the nation."

Pennsylvania Community Development & Finance Corporation

Address: 2561 Bernville Road, Reading, PA 19605

Telephone: 610-898-6045

Website: www.pcdfc.com

Kutztown University of Pennsylvania SBDC

Address: Old Main - Room 24 - E Wing, 15200 Kutztown Rd., Kutztown, PA 19530

Telephone: 877- 472-7232

DESCRIPTION OF SERVICES:

The mission of the Kutztown Small Business Development Center is to provide entrepreneurs and small business owners with the knowledge needed to make smart decisions and prosper.

The Kutztown Small Business Development Center offers existing businesses and early-stage entrepreneurs' access to no cost, confidential consulting services, and learning opportunities. We provide services at our outreach offices in Kutztown, Reading, Harrisburg, Exton, Lancaster, and York.

COST OF SERVICES: No cost

Greater Reading Chamber Alliance

Address: 606 Court Street, Reading, PA 19601

Telephone: 610.376.6766

Email: info@GreaterReading.org

DESCRIPTION OF TRAINING SERVICES:

The Greater Reading Chamber Alliance (GRCA) was formed as a result of a strategic alignment of three existing business organizations serving Berks County: Greater Reading Chamber of Commerce & Industry; Greater Reading Economic Partnership; Greater Berks Development Fund. This unique and innovative partnership, which includes a 1,200-member Chamber of Commerce and Berks County's two leading economic development organizations, represents a comprehensive approach to support the business community. The primary mission of the GRCA is to encourage business attraction, business expansion, job creation and business investment to foster and promote a thriving economy throughout Berks County. By aligning the three organizations, the GRCA can provide a more comprehensive set of supports and services and act as the single point of contact for companies looking to locate or expand in Berks County. In addition, through effective and ongoing advocacy efforts, the GRCA represents a powerful voice in promoting policies that foster a more business-friendly environment throughout the region.

Entrepreneurial Exploration – Higher Ed Programming

Biz Idea Challenge

As part of our goal to promote entrepreneurship, GRCA established the Business Idea Challenge. The competition is open to undergraduate students from Albright College, Alvernia University, Kutztown University, Penn State Berks and Reading Area Community College. Students develop a Business Idea Plan using resources provided by the Chamber and submit the comprehensive plan for judging. Finalists are selected to present their pitch to a panel of judges from local business organizations.

They receive valuable feedback from our panel of judges, like Shark Tank on TV. Awards are presented to the winners at a Chamber Board Meeting, where students are celebrated for their product/service ideas. Program is currently being redeveloped – please inquire if you would like to be a part of the newly developed model!

To learn more about any of our talent development initiatives, or our workforce programs, contact Ellen Albright, Director – Workforce Development.

Incumbent Worker Training/ Upskilling

GRCA is a leading provider in customized and public training for our employers. View the comprehensive list of programming available to employers here.

To learn more about our professional training and development offerings, contact Mark Dolinski, VP of Membership & Events.

Talent Attraction

Site selectors, CEOs, hiring managers, and small business owners all seem to be facing one glaring challenge – the ability to find skilled, available, job-ready talent. It is with this in mind that GRCA has made talent attraction marketing a priority, putting Berks County further on the map as a great place to live, work, and play.

PA CareerLink® Berks County

Address: 1920 Kutztown Road, Suite F, Reading, PA 19604

Telephone: 610- 988-1395; Fax (610) 988-1382

Email: info@bccl.org

DESCRIPTION OF TRAINING SERVICES:

PA CareerLink® is the brand name for Pennsylvania's One-Stop workforce development system. PA CareerLink® Berks County was established in 1999 and operates today under the Workforce Innovation and Opportunity Act of 2014. We are also part of the American Job Center Network, as branded by the U.S. Department of Labor.

Trenton, NJ

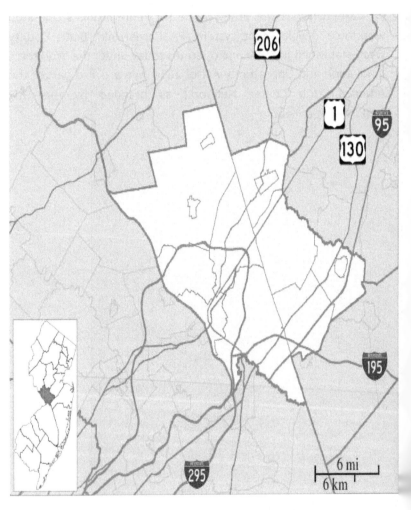

Trenton is the capital city of the U.S. state of New Jersey and the county seat of Mercer County. It briefly served as the capital of the United States in 1784. The city's metropolitan area, consisting of Mercer County, is grouped with the New York Combined Statistical Area by the United States Census Bureau, but it directly borders the Philadelphia metropolitan area and was from 1990 until 2000 part of the Philadelphia Combined Statistical Area. As of the 2010 United States Census, Trenton had a population of 84,913, making it the state's 10th-largest municipality after having been the state's ninth-largest municipality in 2000. The population declined by 490 (-0.6%) from the 85,403 counted in the 2000 Census, which had in turn declined by 3,272 (-3.7%) from the 88,675 counted in the 1990 Census. The Census Bureau's Population Estimates Program calculated that the city's population was 83,203 in 2019, ranking as the 413th largest incorporated place in the nation.

Trenton was a major manufacturing center in the late 19th and early 20th centuries. One relic of that era is the slogan "Trenton Makes, The World Takes", which is displayed on the Lower Free Bridge (just north of the Trenton–Morrisville Toll Bridge). The city adopted the slogan in 1917 to represent Trenton's then-leading role as a major manufacturing center for rubber, wire rope, ceramics and cigars. It was home to American Standards largest fixture factory.

Portions of Trenton are part of an Urban Enterprise Zone. The city was selected in 1983 as one of the initial groups of 10 zones chosen to participate in the program. In addition to other benefits to encourage employment within the Zone, shoppers can take advantage of a reduced 3.3125% sales tax rate (half of the 6 5⁄8% rate charged statewide) at eligible merchants. Established in January 1986, the city's Urban Enterprise Zone status expires in December 2023.

The UEZ program in Trenton and four others original UEZ cities had been allowed to lapse as of January 1, 2017, after Governor Chris Christie, who called the program an "abject failure", vetoed a compromise bill that would have extended the status for two years.[96] In May 2018, Governor Phil Murphy signed a law that reinstated the program in these five cities and extended the expiration date in other zones.

Organizations

NEW JERSEY COMMUNITY CAPITAL

Address: 108 Church Street, 3rd Floor, New Brunswick, NJ 08901

Telephone: 732.640.2061; Fax: 732.543.1201

DESCRIPTION OF SERVICES:

Based in Trenton, New Jersey Community Capital is a 501(c)3 nonprofit, mission-driven lender that works to transform at-risk communities through strategic investments of capital and knowledge. The organization invests in affordable housing, community facilities, and economic development ventures that strengthen neighborhoods, improve education, and increase jobs — ultimately providing greater opportunities for the low-income residents of these communities.

TYPE OF FINANCING OFFERED:

Increasing economic empowerment and opportunities for employment in low-income communities requires a range of investments, from small businesses to larger job generators. NJCC has taken a diverse approach to investing in economic development that has produced almost 6,000 jobs in communities of need.

One such approach is the investment of New Markets Tax Credits (NMTCs). Since 2003, when NJCC was one of the earliest recipients of an NMTC allocation, it has invested over $60 million in NMTCs into a diverse set of projects.

NJCC also continues to increase its investment into small businesses. Foremost among its investments is NJCC's REBUILD New Jersey program, a low-interest disaster recovery loan fund that has helped almost 40 small businesses recover from the impacts of Hurricane Sandy and has recharged their communities.

New Jersey Economic Development Authority

Address: 36 W. State Street, Trenton, NJ 08608

Telephone: 609-858-6700

DESCRIPTION OF SERVICES:

Premier Lender Program

Small Business Fund

Creditworthy small, minority-owned or women-owned businesses in New Jersey that have been in operation for at least one full year and may not have the ability to get bank financing, or not-for-profit corporations that have been operating for at least three full years, may be eligible for assistance under the Small Business Fund.

Direct Loans

New Jersey businesses in need of financing and committed to job creation/retention may be eligible for direct loans through the EDA when conventional financing is not available.

Small Business Lease Assistance Program

The Small Business Lease Assistance Program offers reimbursement of a percentage of annual lease payments to for profit businesses and non-profit organizations in eligible areas that plan to lease between 500 sq. ft. – 5,000 sq. ft. of new or additional market-rate, first-floor office, industrial or retail space for a minimum 5-year term.

TYPE OF FINANCING OFFERED:

Premier Lender Program

Small Business Fund

Direct Loans

Small Business Lease Assistance Program

LOAN RANGES:

Premier Lender Program- Up to $2 million loan participation or $1.5 million loan guarantee for fixed assets

---

Up to $750,000 loan participation or $1.5 million loan guarantee for term working capital.

Up to $750,000 line of credit guarantee.

Direct Loans- Up to $2 million for fixed assets *

Up to $750,000 for working capital

Small Business Fund- Small businesses: Up to $500,000

Not-for-profits: Up to $500,000 with 1.0X historical debt service coverage

Small Business Lease Program- Incentive

Reimbursement of 15% of annual lease payment (for 2 years of a 5 or 10-year lease)

Isles Community Enterprises

Address: 10 Wood Street, Trenton, NJ 08618

Telephone: 609-341-4731

Trenton Business Assistance Corporation

Address: 3111 Quakerbridge Road, Hamilton, NJ 08619

Telephone: 609-587-1133

City of Trenton Division of Economic Development

Address: 319 East State Street, Trenton, NJ 08608

Telephone: 609-989-3504; Fax: 609-989-4243

DESCRIPTION OF SERVICES:

The City of Trenton's Division of Economic Development works to promote business attraction, retention and expansion, with special attention paid to job growth and an increase of city ratables. The Division supports the business community in coordination with organizations and other governmental agencies including the State of New Jersey, County of Mercer, Trenton Downtown Association and various chambers of commerce to further economic development.

Our Services and Programs

Start-Up and Relocation Assistance

The City of Trenton assists incoming businesses through the process of start-up or relocation including business plan review, business training, site selection, PARC consultation, business licensing, inspections and connection with various incentives. If you would like to speak to somebody on relocating or starting your business in Trenton, email emaywar@trentonnj.org.

GROW NJ

The City of Trenton can assist incoming businesses and current Trenton businesses with their continued presence in the City by helping Trenton business take full advantage of State Grow NJ tax credits.

Community Working Groups

In 2016, we replaced the long-standing Trenton Business Week with the Trenton Innovation Project, bringing together 95 Trenton businesses and citizens to define community-designed projects in the areas of Manufacturing, the Arts Economy, Shopping Local, Food Entrepreneurship, Downtown Consumer Traffic and Waterfront Activation. If you would like to join one of these groups, email emaywar@trentonnj.org.

Brownfield Management

Due to Trenton's strong industrial history, the Division is dedicated to environmental issues and Brownfield projects. Through its efforts, the Division is able to meet the many challenges associated with these projects and revitalize old industrial sites into vibrant residential locations, pristine green spaces and parks or thriving business zones. Please click on Brownfield Program for more information regarding this initiative.

Tourism and Culture

The City of Trenton has a rich history. From the American Revolution to the City's strong industrial history of "Trenton Makes, The World Takes", Trenton has stood in the forefront of the growth and development of America. The Division of Economic Development looks to promote this past and works with several organizations and City Departments in marketing and showcasing these hidden treasures.

Urban Enterprise Zone (UEZ)

The New Jersey Legislature created the Urban Enterprise Zone Program in 1983 to help stimulate new economic activity and reduce unemployment within the boundaries of each zone. Trenton was awarded its UEZ designation in 1985. Since that time, the program has successfully served over 800 businesses that have invested millions of dollars in the construction and rehabilitation of new office, commercial and retail space, sports complexes, and other improvements to the city's landscape.

Camden, NJ

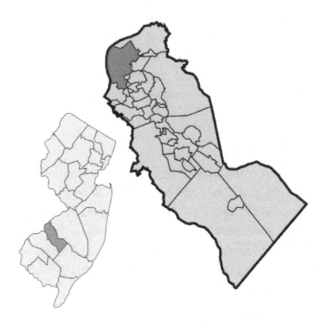

Camden County is a county located in the U.S. state of New Jersey. Its county seat is Camden. As of the 2019 Census estimate, the county's population was 506,471, making it the state's 8th-largest county, representing a 1.4% decrease from the 513,657 enumerated at the 2010 Census, in turn having increased by 4,725 (up 0.9%, the third-lowest growth rate in the state) from the 508,932 counted in the 2000 Census. The most populous place was Camden, with 77,344 residents at the time of the 2010

Census, while Winslow Township covered 58.19 square miles (150.7 km2), the largest total area of any municipality.

The 2010 United States Census counted 513,657 people, 190,980 households, and 129,866 families in the county. The population density was 2,321.5 inhabitants per square mile (896.3/km2). There were 204,943 housing units at an average density of 926.2 per square mile (357.6/km2). The racial makeup was 65.29% (335,389) White, 19.55% (100,441) Black or African American, 0.31% (1,608) Native American, 5.11% (26,257) Asian, 0.03% (165) Pacific Islander, 7.08% (36,354) from other races, and 2.62% (13,443) from two or more races. Hispanic or Latino of any race were 14.24% (73,124) of the population.

Based on data from the Bureau of Economic Analysis, Camden County had a gross domestic product (GDP) of $23.8 billion in 2018, which was ranked 11th in the state and represented an increase of 2.5% from the previous year.

Organizations

Cooperative Business Assistance Corporation

Address: 328 Market Street, Camden, NJ 08102

Telephone: 866-966-8181

Website: www.cbaclenders.com

DESCRIPTION OF SERVICES:

Cooperative Business Assistance Corporation (CBAC) is a nonprofit organization providing market or below market interest rate business loans and technical assistance to small businesses located in or moving into the Philadelphia, Pennsylvania and Southern New Jersey region.

CBAC is a Community Development Financial Institution, and a Community Development Entity as recognized by the United States Department of the Treasury. We are also recognized by the United States Small Business Administration (SBA) as a designated intermediary lender for their Micro Loan, and Associate Development Company for SBA 504 Programs.

TYPE OF FINANCING OFFERED:

Micro Loan Program

Micro Loans Demonstration Program combines the resources and experience of the U.S. Small Business Administration and CBAC in providing small loans and technical assistance to small businesses. Under the Microloan Program, the SBA makes funds available to CBAC and they use the funds to make loans to new and existing small businesses.

Under the Microloan Program, a small business can borrow up to $50,000 directly from CBAC or up to $105,000 in partnership with other lenders.

1.   Eligibility Requirements

Virtually any type of for-profit small business is eligible for the Microloan Program. It must, however, meet the SBAs size standards at the time of application.

2.   Use of Loan Funds

Microloan funds may be used for working capital or to purchase inventory, supplies, machinery, equipment, furniture, and fixtures. These funds may not be used to purchase real estate or provide for down payments on equipment or vehicles otherwise leased or financed by others. With limited exceptions, the funds cannot be used to refinance existing debts.

3.   Loan Terms

Under the Microloan Program, the maximum direct loan amount is $50,000 with the average loan around $15,000. The maximum loan amount in partnership with other lenders is $105,000. The maximum loan term is six years. Loan term varies according to loan size and use of funds. Under the Microloan Program, CBAC offers favorable interest rates.

4.   Collateral Requirements

CBAC sets collateral requirements in accordance with credit standards for the MicroLoan Program. In most cases, loans are at least partially collateralized by equipment, contracts, inventory or other property. CBAC also requires personal guaranties.

U.S. Small Business Administration 504 Program

The U.S. Small Business Administration through CBAC enables growing businesses to secure long-term, fixed-rate financing for major fixed assets through its 504 Program. It is designed to promote local economic development by helping healthy, growing businesses finance the acquisition of long-term fixed assets, such as land, building, modernizing, renovating or restoring of facilities. These assets must be used principally to enable the business to create or retain jobs.

504 Facts for Small Businesses

If you are a healthy business whose expansion plans call for the investment and use of real estate or equipment, you may qualify for up to 90% financing through the 504 Loan Program.

Here are the 504 advantages:

• Low down payment - you conserve valuable operating capital

• Below market fixed rate-no future rate fluctuations

• Long term - brings debt services in line with the cash flow generated by the asset

Typical 504 Financing Structure

Projected Costs	Source	Lien	Funding Limits	Rate	Term Real Estate	Term Equipment
50%	Financial Institution	1st	No Limits	Market	10 years or Longer	7 years or Longer
40%	504	2nd	Min: $50,000	Fixed		
			Max: $2,000,000-$4,000,000	Fixed	20 years	10 years

Loan Terms

Interest rates are based on the current market rate for 5-year and 10-year U.S. Treasury issues, plus an amount slightly above the Treasury rate. Maturities of 10 and 20 years are available. Repayment is made in monthly, level-debt installments.

Fees

CBAC's fees cannot exceed the 1.5 percent processing fee on the SBA's debenture. A monthly servicing fee, of not less than 0.5

percent and not move than 2 percent per year, is paid on the unpaid debenture balance to CBAC.

There are also fees to cover the cost of public issuance of securities, fees paid to the SBA for its guaranty, and a one-time fee to the senior lienholder.

Eligibility

An eligible business must be a for-profit corporation, partnership or proprietorship with a net worth (including any affiliates) of $6 million or less. Average net profits after taxes cannot exceed $2 million per year for the previous two years.

Applying for a Loan

You can download the application or contact Cooperative Business any time Monday through Friday between 8:30 am and 5:00 pm to speak to a loan officer and request personalized assistance.

Financing Opportunities for Camden And Southern New Jersey

Commercial Loans from $35,000 to $500,000 are available for new enterprises and existing businesses located in Southern New Jersey. These loans generally have a five year term, and have a fixed rate of interest. The loans may be used to purchase equipment, inventory, minor leasehold improvements, or for working capital. New business owners are required to complete entrepreneurial training and write a business plan. All loans are personally guaranteed by the owners, and the lenders take the best available collateral.

Fixed Asset Loans are available to businesses with at least two years of positive operating experience located in Southern New Jersey. Loans up to $500,000 are available. These loans have up to a twenty year term and have a fixed rate of interest set on a deal by deal basis. CBAC requires that for every dollar it lends, the borrower leverages an additional two dollars. The leveraged portion generally comes from other lenders, the borrower's bank of account, and the New Jersey Economic Development Authority (NJEDA). All loans are personally guaranteed by the owners, and the lenders take the best available collateral. CBAC's loans are subordinated to the other lenders. Borrowers may use these funds for permanent mortgages for commercial real estate acquisition, repairs, equipment purchases, and up to 25% may be used for working capital.

Loan Guaranty Program provides a guarantee up to 40 % of a conventional bank loan or $75,000 whichever is less. The guaranty program is proposed to help small businesses in Southern New Jersey establish banking relationships and fill gaps left by other guaranty programs. The loan guarantees coincide with bank terms and have a ten-year maximum term.

Small Business Emergency Loan Program assists Camden businesses in times of fiscal or physical crisis. The Fund makes small loans at low interest rate based on repayment ability for emergency purposes such as immediate building and equipment repair and catastrophic financial problems. Terms are generally five years or less. The loans are generally capped at $6,000 and this program is only available in Camden City.

Financing Opportunities for Cumberland County

Loans up to $500,000 are available to businesses with an operating history and/or a well-documented business plan with financial projections that demonstrate the ability to repay the loan. These loans have up to a twenty year term and have a fixed rate of interest set on a deal by deal basis. CBAC requires that for every dollar it lends, the borrower leverages an additional two dollars. The leveraged portion generally comes from other lenders, the borrower's bank of account, and the New Jersey Economic Development Authority (NJEDA). All loans are personally guaranteed by the owners, and the lenders take the best available collateral. CBAC's loans are generally subordinated to the other lenders. Borrowers may use these funds for permanent mortgages for commercial real estate acquisition, repairs, equipment purchases, and working capital. Additionally, loans are available under the United States Rural Development program.

COST OF FINANCING (FEES): 75.00 non-refundable application contribution is due when submitting this application and must be payable to CBAC.

Camden County Improvement Authority

Address: 2220 Voorhees Town Center. Voorhees, NJ 08043

Telephone: 856-968-7100

Email: justask@camdencounty.com

DESCRIPTION OF SERVICES:

The Camden County Improvement Authority is an independent, public agency created by the Camden County Board of Freeholders to provide low-cost financing, economic development and project development services for local units, community organizations, and not-for-profit entities to foster economic, employment, redevelopment and affordable housing development projects that improve the quality of life for the residents of Camden County and other eligible areas of the State of New Jersey.

TYPE OF FINANCING OFFERED:

New Jersey Smart Start Clean Energy Programs

New Jersey's Clean Energy Program is making renewable energy technologies like solar, wind, and biomass affordable, practical, and plain smart! The Clean Energy Program, administered by New

Jersey's Office of Clean Energy, offers commercial, industrial, and municipal customers financial incentives, design support, and technical assistance to integrate energy efficient and renewable energy technologies into new construction, upgrades, and new cooling & heating equipment installations.

New Jersey SmartStart Buildings Program

New Jersey's SmartStart Building Program is administered by New Jersey's Office of Clean Energy. Whether you are starting a commercial or industrial project from the ground up, renovating existing space, or upgrading equipment, New Jersey has unique opportunities to upgrade the quality of the project.

There are several improvement options for commercial, industrial, institutional, government, and agricultural projects throughout New Jersey. Alternatives are designed to enhance quality – while building in energy efficiency to save money now and for many years to come!

Project categories included in this program are New Construction and Additions, Renovations, Remodeling and Equipment Replacement.

For more detailed information on the program and eligibility requirements, please contact a New Jersey's Clean Energy Program Customer Service Representative at 1-866-NJSMART (1-866-657-6278) or go to New Jersey's Clean Energy Site.

Sustainable Development Loan Fund

If your company is going green, you could be eligible for government financing to help you improve the environmental quality of your operation. The Sustainable Development Loan Fund offers low interest loans up to $500,000 for businesses that support and advance sustainable actions such as:

- Production processes which draw raw materials from environmentally sustainable sources
- Pollution prevention
- Production of finished products that are recyclable and have a minor or positive environmental impact.

Smart Growth Redevelopment Funding

If your business is planning to redevelop a commercial, industrial, office or mixed-use site in an urban or developed suburb, you could be eligible for up to $1 million in funding for site preparation costs. This includes:

- Land assemblage
- Demolition
- Removal of materials and debris
- Engineering costs

Projects must have municipal support and be part of a local development plan.

Municipalities may also apply for long-term, low-interest financing for projects in municipality-designated redevelopment areas. Bonds are secured by payments in lieu of taxes (PILOT) agreements negotiated by the municipality and developer, special assessments on property benefiting from the improvements, or both. Qualifying bonds may be excluded from the municipality's gross debt. For more information email justask@camdencounty.com.

Brownfields Redevelopment Financing

There are several former industrial properties in Camden County and in our urban areas with existing infrastructure already in place, including proximity to roads, highways, and public transportation. The Camden County Business Team can help you gain access to many very low-interest loans, incentives, grants and creative tax structures for various stages of the Brownfields restoration process from planning, to remediation, to development.

Camden City Brownfields & Contaminated Site Remediation Program (BCSRP)

The reimbursement fund offers financial incentives for businesses and developers to clean-up and redevelop contaminated sites. Developers can qualify for up to $250,000 and in special cases up to $500,000. Reimbursement is up to 75% of the cost as provided by the program guidelines.

New Jersey Environmental Infrastructure Trust Programs (NJEIT)

New Jersey Environmental loan leader for 21 years provides blended rate and low-rate loans for many aspects of redevelopment projects. Brownfields loans are set at as low as 50% of market rate for a 20-year term; target area smart-growth loans up to 75% market rate. Restrictions apply. NJEIT also funds wastewater, landfill, and drinking water projects.

Hazardous Discharge Site Remediation Loan Program

The Hazardous Discharge Site Remediation Fund provides funding to public entities, businesses and non-profit organizations for the investigation and remediation of a suspected or known discharge of a hazardous substance. Administered through a partnership between the New Jersey Department of Environmental Protection and the New Jersey Economic Development Authority, qualified applicants could receive loans in varying amounts:

• Up to $1 million in loans or loan guarantees for up to 10 years.

• Up to $2 million in grants and loans to municipalities.

- Up to 25% of project costs in matching grants to individuals.

The Camden County Business Team can help guide you to all available options. Just ask!

Resources:

- DEP Site Remediation Requirements Checklist

- Hazardous Discharge Site Remediation Fund Loans & Grants Available Pursuant to S-277

Cooperative Business Assistance Corporation

Address: 328 Market Street · Camden, NJ 08102

Telephone: 856- 966-8181; Fax: 856- 966-0036

DESCRIPTION OF SERVICES:

Cooperative Business can offer you technical assistance. Cooperative Business for technical assistance for a new or expanding business. In order to receive the full benefit of technical assistance you must be willing to make a one to three-month investment of your time.

- As a resource for professionals and firms who work with small businesses.

- Setting up a financial bookkeeping system.

- Designing a marketing strategy.

- As a resource for government programs and regulations.

- Locating sources to hire a qualified workforce.

- Evaluating financial performance.

Rutgers University

Address: Office of Economic Development, 303 Cooper St., Camden, NJ 08102

Telephone: 856- 225-6388

DESCRIPTION OF SERVICES:

The Office of Economic Development seeks to develop opportunities to engage new audiences in the growth of our host city, and to increase Rutgers–Camden's services to the State of New Jersey and the City of Camden.

The office works to build relationships with a wide range of businesses and organizations with the goal of enhancing the economy of the greater Camden region. Based on the successful models of other urban universities, the Rutgers–Camden Office of Economic Development seeks to encourage retail growth and other forms of investment in our neighborhood and city by:

- Utilizing the intellectual and physical assets of Rutgers to support and grow the economic development activity in Camden and neighboring regions.

- Partnering with public, private, and non-profit organizations with a shared goal of creating a knowledge-based economy that will attract businesses that support and benefit from the research and activities at Rutgers–Camden.

- Strengthening the relationships between local industries and academia.

•   Promoting the current and potential workforce in the region.

•   Participating in strategic neighborhood revitalization efforts in the City of Camden.

•   Seeking to improve the economic well-being and quality of life of the City of Camden.

New Jersey Small Business Development Center (SBDC) at Rutgers – Camden

Address: 419 Cooper Street, Camden, NJ 08102

Telephone: 856-225-6221

DESCRIPTION OF SERVICES:

The New Jersey Small Business Development Centers network helps New Jersey's small businesses succeed. The statewide office, headquartered at Rutgers–Newark, serves all 21 New Jersey counties through regional centers and affiliate offices. The Small Business Development Center at Rutgers–Camden is the southern region's primary office.

Camden County Improvement Authority

Address: 2220 Voorhees Town Center, Voorhees, NJ 08043

Telephone: 856-566-3105

Email: chris.orlando@camdencounty.com

DESCRIPTION OF TRAINING SERVICES:

The Camden County Improvement Authority is an independent, public agency created by the Camden County Board of Freeholders to provide low cost financing, economic development and project development services for local units, community organizations, and not-for-profit entities to foster economic, employment, redevelopment and affordable housing development projects that improve the quality of life for the residents of Camden County and other eligible areas of the State of New Jersey.

COST OF TRAINING SERVICES:

Camden County is among the world's best-connected regions. Thanks to world-class infrastructure, a well-educated and skilled workforce, high quality of life with nationally ranked colleges and communities steeped with rich cultural experiences- Camden County truly has it all!

Camden County's Economic Development and Business Services Team is here to help...JUST ASK!

The team is comprised of a variety of agencies that administer programs designed to help your business or organization thrive in Camden County.   Services Include:

- Site selection and relocation

- Financing and incentives

- Workforce and training grants and programs

- Small and mid-size business services

State (Commonwealth of Pennsylvania)

Technical Assistance

- PA Business One-Stop Shop

- Business Resources for Veterans

- Defense Industry Assistance

- Local Business Assistance

- Technology Innovation

- Broadband Resources

- Manufacturing PA Initiative

- Workforce Development

State (Delaware)

Operating since 1984, the SBDC is dedicated to helping new and scaling businesses grow and prosper within Delaware and the region by providing no or low-cost advisory and training services. The SBDC is the only statewide, nationally accredited program that provides high quality one-on-one consulting, training and information resources to help small businesses grow and succeed. The SBDC program is a public/private partnership with the U.S. Small Business Administration, the State of Delaware and the University of Delaware. The SBDC also has its own Procurement Technical Assistance Center to help existing businesses break into and make sense of government procurement by identifying and preparing bids on contracts with all levels of government as well as prime contractors.

State (New Jersey)

New Jersey Economic Development Authority-

If you are a business in need of financing to grow in New Jersey, a not-for-profit organization seeking capital to expand community services, a municipality looking to attract a major corporation within your boundaries, or a developer requiring funds for a major redevelopment project, the New Jersey Economic Development Authority (EDA) is ready to put its resources to work for you.

With our large portfolio of varied programs and services, the EDA can assist you with access to capital, including tax-exempt and taxable bond financing, loans, loan guarantees, and business and tax incentives. In addition, we offer real estate development assistance and state-of-the-art technology facilities like the Technology Centre of New Jersey in North Brunswick.

Small & Mid-Sized Business

The EDA has a long history of supporting growth in New Jersey for businesses of all sizes, but support of small to mid-sized businesses has always been one of our top priorities. With the creative and versatile loan solutions available to small to mid-sized businesses through the EDA, now is an opportune time to contact EDA to determine if any of our programs may be the right fit for your small to mid-sized business needs.

Access

Access is a pilot lending program that provides financing to small businesses in New Jersey - either in the form of direct loans through EDA, or through loan participations or guarantees in partnership with an EDA Premier Lender.

Access is different from other EDA financing programs in that it provides greater flexibility to borrowers by placing greater emphasis on the borrower's cash flow and less emphasis on hard collateral.

Premier Lender Program

The Premier Lender Program creates new opportunities for small businesses and EDA's lending partners by providing new, low-cost financing opportunities with faster turnaround.

If your small business is discussing potential financing with one of EDA's Premier Lender banks, EDA's participation or guarantee of a portion of the financing can lower the cost of borrowing for your business.

Direct Loans

New Jersey businesses in need of financing and committed to job creation/retention may be eligible for direct loans through EDA when financing is not available under other EDA financing programs.

Small Business Bonding Readiness Assistance Program

New Jersey Economic Development Authority (NJEDA) has partnered with The African American Chamber of Commerce of New Jersey (AACCNJ) for the Small Business Bonding Readiness Assistance Program. The program is designed to help construction business needs, providing comprehensive technical assistance, supportive services and access to capital.

Small Business Fund

Creditworthy small, minority-owned or women-owned businesses in New Jersey that have been in operation for at least one full year and may not have the ability to get bank financing, or not-for-profit corporations that have been operating for at least three full years, may be eligible for direct loans under the Small Business Fund.

Small Business Lease Assistance Program

The Small Business Lease Assistance Program offers reimbursement of a percentage of annual lease payments to for profit businesses and non-profit organizations in eligible areas that plan to lease between 500 sq. ft. – 5,000 sq. ft. of new or additional market-rate, first-floor office, industrial or retail space for a minimum 5-year term.

Garden State Growth Zone Business Improvement Incentive

The Garden State Growth Zone (GSGZ) Business Improvement Incentive (BII) offers grants of up to 50% of total project cost, grant amount not to exceed $20,000, to businesses operating within the first-floor of a commercial corridor in the GSGZ that are planning to make building improvements, with a minimum project cost of $5,000.

Small Business Services

In addition to the millions of dollars in funding EDA administers as loans and loan guarantees to New Jersey small businesses, EDA also partners with several organizations that provide a wide array of services to New Jersey small businesses and entrepreneurs.

Wineries & Vineyards

Eligible New Jersey wineries and vineyards can now access financing through the NJEDA.

About the Author:

Calvin R. Tucker, President & CEO, Eagles Capital Advisors, LLC, a financial, management & Economic Development Consultant firm, is the Deputy Chairman, Pennsylvania Republican Party and serves as a consultant/Capital Manager, West Philadelphia Financial Services Institution (WPFSI). Mr. Tucker has written several articles and blogs on small businesses and education in the minority community which appeared in the WPFSI monthly newsletter, Philadelphia Daily News and in the Mt. Airy Patch On-Line Newspaper.

Mr. Tucker is a former cohost of WPFSI Radio Show, There's Money Out There", which aired on WURD 900 AM every third

Saturday of month. Mr. Tucker graduated from Lincoln University in 1975 with a BA in Business Administration and Finance. He also did post graduate work toward his MBA at LaSalle University. Mr. Tucker has over 30 years of business experience, particularly in the financial services industry working with all types of business entities; both large, medium and small. Mr. Tucker has served as an Executive and Senior Officer of several financial institutions, such as Advance Bank, United Bank of Philadelphia, GMAC Commercial Mortgage Corporation (United States, Canada and France) where he originated and closed well over $750 million in loan transactions. He was a Regional & National Director of the Resolution Trust Corporation where he managed, liquidated and closed numerous banking institutions and receivership assets. Mr. Tucker also owned and managed several family businesses, such as International Mailing Technologies, Inc and C. R. Tucker Associates.

In addition to Mr. Tucker's business experience, he has served on numerous boards, such as Presbyterian Children Village, West Philadelphia Culture Center-Paul Robeson House, African American Chamber of Commerce, Entrepreneurs Works (formerly Community Capital Works), Habitat for Humanity Philadelphia, White Dog Enterprises, Philadelphia Board of Public Assistance and the University of Pennsylvania Real Estate Society. He is also a former member of the Vesper Club, current member of the Pennsylvania Commonwealth Club, and past member of Near Equity Fund of Women's Opportunity Resource Center.

Made in the USA
Middletown, DE
11 March 2021